Table of *Jou*

DEDICATION	3
ACKNOWLEDGEMENTS	4
FORWARD	6
PROLOGUE	7
CHAPTER 1 - THE BEGINNING OF THIS JOURNEY	10
CHAPTER 2 - TRIP TO VENEZUELA	18
CHAPTER 3 – PUERTO AYACUCHO	24
CHAPTER 4 - TRIP UPRIVER	32
CHAPTER 5 - PIAROA TRIBE AND THE FINDLEYS	38
CHAPTER 6 - PUNTA PIAROA	46
CHAPTER 7 - THE "RINGING OF THE BELLS"	58
CHAPTER 8 - RETURNING TO SAN JUAN AS A FAMILY	64
CHAPTER 9 - PLANE CRASH - TRAGEDY HITS	72

Journey into the Unknown

CHAPTER 10 – DEATH BRINGS LIFE	82
CHAPTER 11 – CHANGES AND TIME OUT	90
CHAPTER 12 – NEW OPEN DOORS	96
CHAPTER 13 – FIRST CONTACT	106
CHAPTER 14 – MOVE INTO PARGUAZA RIVER AREA	114
CHAPTER 15 – BACK TO SAN JUAN	130
CHAPTER 16 - TROUBLING TIMES	140
CHAPTER 17 – TRANSLATION	150
CHAPTER 18 - A CHANGE OF MINISTRY	164
CHAPTER 19 – MISSIONARY TRAINING INSTITUTE	182
CHAPTER 20 – CFM IN ACTION	194
CHAPTER 21 – THE FINAL LAP OF THIS JOURNEY	204
EPILOGUE	214

Journey into the Unknown

Dedication

I dedicate this book to my grandchildren: Amanda, Brianna, Alaina and Carter Findley. I often desired that one day they would be able to visit and see the people with whom Fred and I lived and worked. Since that never happened, I hope this book will give them a glimpse into the lives of those who became like family and a country that is a second home to us.

Journey into the Unknown

Acknowledgements

Writing a book about my life over a span of sixty plus years was harder than I ever imagined when I started this new adventure. I would not have had the courage to do it without the help that several people have given me. The first of which is my dear neighbor, Debbie Diss. I will be forever thankful for her tireless and selfless sacrifice of time helping me put this book together. Also, I am grateful for Brian, her husband, for his patience with our ever-changing schedules while working on this book.

A special thank you to Davey Jank, the son of one of our co-workers in Venezuela, who later served as a missionary, along with his wife Marie. Davey is also an author and a great editor. He helped me greatly by going through the manuscript and making many suggestions. Also, a special thanks to others who read through the final script and noted any mistakes found.

To my children, Melanie, Brian and Jody Findley, I am grateful for their being a part of my life and this book. Not only were they a part of the story, but they used the abilities God has given them to help me with suggestions, proofreading, and especially my struggles with the computer. I could have never done it without them.

To my loving husband, Fred, better known by the Venezuelans as "Perico", I thank for his patience with me and with the flood of questions I regularly asked him. I also thank him for his continual encouragement to not give up when I felt that I couldn't go on any longer. We felt a lot of different emotions as we read through letters written

Journey into the Unknown

between 1954 to 2005. We reminisced over many things with tears of joy and sorrow as well as thankfulness for God's protection when we had no idea that we were in danger. We are also thankful that, at times, God didn't let us have what we really wanted and for which we had asked; we later found that God had something much better in store for us.

We thank God for His Faithfulness as we made this journey together serving Him.

"GREAT IS THY FAITHFULNESS, O GOD OUR FATHER"

Journey into the Unknown

Forward

In 2008, we moved next door to Fred and Barbara Findley. They were kind, generous, helping neighbors, and we quickly became friends. Barbara told us later she had been praying God would move Christians in to the house next door to them. And there we were! A year after that, we found out Barbara felt God wanted her to write a book, but she was praying for someone to help her get organized. And there we were! Watch out for Barbara's prayers!

When we sifted through information from letters Barbara used to put her book together, my husband and I were blessed and encouraged with how God used their family in Venezuela to accomplish His intricate and magnificent will. My husband and I thank God for the privilege of being friends with Barbara and Fred, because our friendship has allowed us to hear and read about their experiences, which are a testimony of His amazing faithfulness and love.

To God be the glory! Great things He has done!

Debbie Diss

Journey into the Unknown

Prologue

While returning home from an upriver village with a visiting couple and their two small boys, the wife shocked me with this question, "why don't you write a book?" She seemingly was going through some culture shock as she transferred from the modern city of Caracas to the remote jungles of the Amazon. She was asking questions most of the time and was in awe of what all they were seeing for the first time. We had just left the village of Guayavalito where the Piaroas were having one of the typical festivals.

This happened in the mid 70's and was the beginning of our being asked the same question many times. I could never forget that question and it became prominent in my mind when we were leaving Venezuela for the last time. Some of the church leaders asked us if we would put in writing the story of God's work in their country and with the Piaroa tribe, how the Gospel first came to them and what change it made in their lives. They wanted, in writing, the experiences of the early missionaries as they took the Gospel to unreached indigenous people.

The excuse that I always gave those who asked was, "I am not a writer" or "maybe someday after we retire." I never desired to write a book, nor did I know how to start. How could I possibly remember things that happened almost fifty years ago? I never kept a diary. This didn't seem to change the feeling in my heart that I should at least be willing to pray about this. This feeling became even stronger when we finally moved back to the U.S. and were settled in our first home in our homeland. As we unpacked our things, we had left stored at my parent's house, I came

Journey into the Unknown

across all the letters that I had written to my Mom and Dad from the first time I left for Venezuela as a single missionary until after our first child was born. Later my Mother-in-law came to me with a shoe box full of letters and asked if I wanted them. She was getting ready to throw them away if I didn't want them. They were letters that she had written to her family and Fred's Aunt had saved them from the time they first went to Venezuela in 1954 until she returned to the States in the mid-70's. Also, included in the shoe box were all the letters that we had written to her until we returned in 2005. Several times I was tempted to throw them away as I needed to start "downsizing," but I just couldn't do it. The thought of a book kept coming back to me.

A few years ago, our neighbors, invited us over to their house for a cook-out along with a few other people from the neighborhood. During our time together, the hostess asked us to introduce ourselves. So, we talked about our years as missionaries in Venezuela. Later on, my neighbor asked the all familiar question, "Barbara, why don't you write a book?" I thought, "Oh, there we go again." I used my well-worn answer, "I am not a writer, I do not know how to even start." The difference this time is that I had been praying that if it was the Lord's will for me to write a book that He would send someone who would offer to help me. My neighbor answered immediately, "I will help you; I have helped a friend type a book." Wow, did I just get an answer!! Remember the letters?

So, this book was born.

Journey into the Unknown

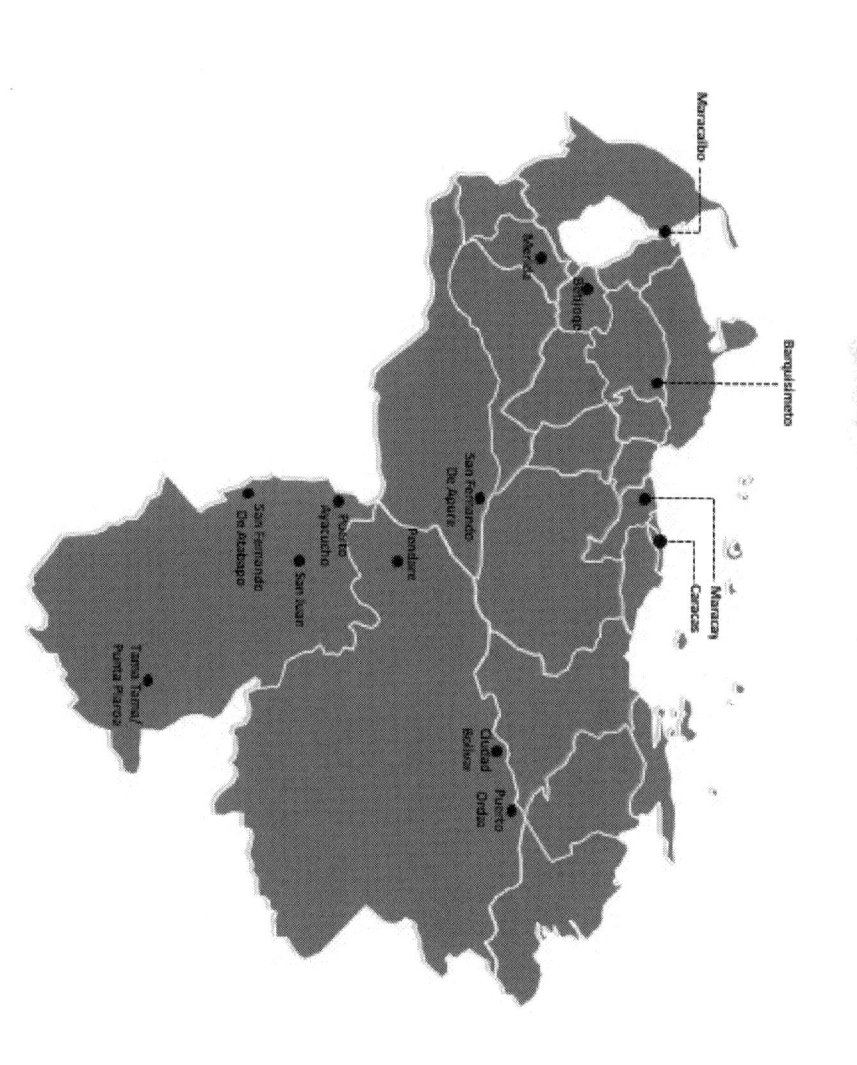

Map of Venezuela with Locations

Journey into the Unknown

Chapter 1 - The Beginning of this Journey

I was born on July 15, 1939 and raised in a Christian home by parents who loved and served the Lord. Horace and Elsie Wilson were used by the Lord to be a part of the founding members of Grace Gospel Church in Huntington, West Virginia. They tell me I was only five days old when they had the first service in the church. My brothers David and Norman were two and six.

I grew up in the church and learned God's Word from a young age. My mother was one of the Sunday School teachers, and I learned much from her there and at home. She led me to the Lord when I was very young. I also learned at a young age that as a Christian we were told to take the Gospel to the entire world. We had yearly missionary conferences, and they were the highlight of the year at our church. We hosted many of the missionaries in our home. I loved them all and spent a lot of time asking about the mission field and the people who never had the chance to hear about God and His Son who died for our sins.

Barbara With Siblings

I remember, particularly, one elderly missionary. He was never too busy to pay attention to my two brothers and me.

The Beginning of this Journey

We called him Grandpa Prinzing. I remember I asked him one question after another about the native people. I am sure he was tired of my talking all the time, but I was insistent. We had another missionary stay with us, and he taught me to swim. I believe those early years of my life and exposure to missions was one of the things the Lord used in leading me into foreign missionary work.

As the years passed, unbeknownst to me, God was preparing me for missions. The stories of all these missionaries touched my heart. I started to feel a burden for people who had never had a chance to hear the gospel and believe in Jesus Christ. As I neared my graduation from high school in 1957, I knew that I needed to have some Bible School and Missions training first. My oldest brother David was attending Providence Bible College in Providence, Rhode Island. On one of his school breaks, he brought home a good friend and classmate. When we found out that Roland Bixby was also preparing to be a missionary, we listened with great interest when he talked about New Tribes Mission (NTM), where he was planning to train for work with indigenous tribal people.

Later a young lady, who was on her way to Venezuela, visited us. She was also part of NTM. Faye Taylor (Walz) was going to work in a small mission print shop where they printed the first manuscripts translated in some of the tribal languages in both Venezuela and Colombia. Upon learning more about New Tribes Mission and its three stages of training (Bible School, Missionary Training, and Language/Linguistic Training), I felt NTM was an answer to my prayers. This was where I would go to prepare for the work the Lord had laid on my heart from a young age.

Journey into the Unknown

I left for Milwaukee, Wisconsin, soon after my graduation from high school. This is where I had my first experience of *culture shock*! I went from a southern city in West Virginia where I was born and raised to the big northern city of Milwaukee where I knew no one and understood very little of the culture. My first contact with a different culture had just begun, and as I look back on it, I can see that even in this God was preparing me for the future.

This is where my first case of homesickness occurred also! I was so homesick, that at one point, I begged the leadership to let me go back home to West Virginia. The Lord didn't forget about me though. He brought in to my life a fellow student, Dawn Sammons (Christopher). At the institute, Dawn was moving in to start Bible School a year after me. I offered to help her as she was carrying things from her car up to her room by herself. We immediately became good friends. We were more like sisters. I had met her parents and instantly felt like a member of their family. As time passed, I became very sick with something like pneumonia and being away from home while so sick amplified my homesickness. I wanted to go home! By God's grace, Dawn's parents, Millie and Kootney Sammons, lived close to the school. They found out from Dawn about my homesickness doubled with my pneumonia and asked me to stay with their family for a week to recover. My homesickness and my pneumonia started to subside with their care and love. The Lord had used our friendship and my friend's family to get me through my homesickness. Also, I had a second set of parents…who called me their "rebel daughter," because I was from West Virginia (the South)!

The Beginning of this Journey

After finishing Bible School in Milwaukee, the first of the three phases of NTM training, I was ready to move on to the second stage, near Orlando, Florida, which we called "Boot Camp." Today this is referred to as the "practical" part of missionary training. Here we were taught how to live in a foreign country with their customs and culture. We were taught how to adapt to a completely different way of living. We were taught how to survive in an isolated jungle where the native people had never seen an outsider before and the missionary did not know a word of their language. We also learned how to work with other missionaries and how to deal with problems as they might arise, and many, many more things.

"Boot Camp" was a very intimidating, and yet truly practical, part of my training. In Boot Camp, we learned about simplified medicine, hair cutting, soap making, butchering, gardening, hiking, survival skills, swimming, boating, dietetics and how to make an oven out of items available in the jungle. Based on past missionaries' experiences, we were being prepared to survive in the jungle to do our ministry successfully. We were also trained in how to talk with our fellow missionaries about problems to positively resolve issues as our co-workers were our only fellowship and communication at the beginning of our ministry.

During the Boot Camp training, we were taken away from the school for six weeks for "jungle camp." They sent us to an isolated area where we, as a group, trained for jungle survival. We, the students and some teachers, took with us everything we needed. We took materials we thought we needed to cut down trees, build huts, cook over an open

Journey into the Unknown

fire, etc. We lived for six weeks off the land with no electricity or running water. We found a creek and boiled the water. We made mud ovens. We made beds out of poles we cut in the forest and twine we brought with us. Families with several children made bunk beds out of the trees in the woods. We made tables out of small trees that we split lengthwise, so we could keep supplies off the ground. We brought the main staples (non-perishable) such as beans, rice, oatmeal, etc. In the Florida forest, we didn't have access to jungle fruits to supplement our diet, so we used staples for these six weeks. We learned how to survive in the jungle.

Another aspect of the Boot Camp training, besides classes in the morning, was "work detail" in the afternoon. Single girls work assignments were to clean bathrooms, hold classes for children, help in the nursery, clean classrooms, etc. Men were assigned to maintain the facilities, repair homes in the compound, do rewiring and plumbing, any construction work needed, etc. When they found out I knew how to type, they asked me to work in the office for work detail. I was the only single girl, the other women were mothers, and so their work detail was maintaining their home and caring for their families. Five days a week my work detail was typing in the Boot Camp leader's office. I couldn't wait to move on to the final phase of training, the language/linguistics school. However, when I was close to finishing the Boot Camp phase of training, I encountered an unexpected detour.

The leadership of New Tribes Mission wrote to the leadership at the training school to ask if they would talk to me about taking a year off training. They wanted me to go

The Beginning of this Journey

to the mission headquarters in Woodworth, Wisconsin, to fill in for a lady on sick leave. After they presented the idea to me, they told me to pray about it, as they knew I preferred to continue my NTM training. As I prayed, I was reminded that I had dedicated my life to be used by the Lord in whatever way He would choose. Thinking about that, and with the promise of only a one-year delay, I agreed to accept the position.

I moved back to Wisconsin in 1959 to fill in as a secretary. After being there over a year, I talked with leadership and reminded them that they had asked for only a year's delay. They replied, "when you find a replacement, you can go." That seemed almost impossible at the time. To find someone to come and take this job who wasn't in the mission already and for minimal pay didn't seem likely. However, God had other plans. I was living in a girls' dorm while working as the secretary. We all ate together for our meals. During one of the meals, I told my friends about the situation, and one of the girls said her sister might be interested in this position. So, she asked her, and in just a month or so the Lord had provided a replacement.

In 1960, off I went to the third and final phase of my NTM training, language/linguistics, in Fredonia, Wisconsin. There we were trained in linguistics, language breakdown, how to learn a foreign language, culture, and Bible translation. This training lasted for approximately a year based on the student's progress. As before, we had classes in the morning, work detail in the afternoon, and studying in the evenings. As before, I was placed in an office for my work detail as a secretary/typist. As I neared the end of my third phase of training, the big question we had was what

Journey into the Unknown

country were we going to for our mission field assignment? It seemed like most knew where they were going, but not me. I asked a group of friends to pray that the Lord would show me in some way where I should go. I was torn because from the very beginning I had Venezuela on my mind; however, I was also tempted to go to Panama where my older brother was in missions. I wanted to join him and be with family. At the time, I really felt the importance of knowing God's will and not mine, so I continued to pray about this as I didn't have a definitive answer yet. One day after much prayer, a young couple who were also taking the training with me came to my door and asked to talk to me. They told me that they had been praying for me about this matter, and they felt the Lord was leading them to talk with me about going to Venezuela. That was the answer to my prayers. Venezuela would be my mission field.

The next step was preparing for my departure to Venezuela: deputation, government required paperwork, purchasing and packing items to take, buying tickets and making reservations. This didn't sound too complicated at first, but for some it takes longer than for others. For me, I think, it took almost two years! However, I was finally ready!

I had heard that sometimes when a person gets close to going to the field, Satan tries to discourage or derail them,

The Beginning of this Journey

so they choose not to go. I did not escape this temptation. I had finished my training in 1961, but, as I said earlier, it took two years to prepare for my departure which would eventually be the first part of 1963. In 1962, I visited a church to tell them about my plans and raise support. While there, I met a preacher's son, and we hit it off. We started dating. That turned into falling in love, so we thought, and we were even discussing marriage. I knew in my heart that this was not right, because he did not have the same desire that I had for going to the mission field. He did desire to serve the Lord and planned to go to a very well-known Christian university, but he did not feel God was leading him to the mission field. I knew we had to terminate the relationship since we were on different paths. I remember the last thing he said to me when we were together: "maybe God has someone waiting for you in Venezuela." I politely agreed with him but wasn't very convinced that would be possible. It was a known fact that the ratio of single women to single men on the mission field was ten to one. However, without my knowledge, my mom and one of her close friends had been praying together that God would provide me a soul-mate on the mission field. My mom was a bold prayer warrior; she prayed for a specific man for me. She had read an article that he wrote, and she was very impressed with him. Also, he was one of the very few men available. Nonetheless, I knew meeting someone was nearly impossible. I had settled it in my heart that if the Lord wanted me to be single the rest of my life that was what I was willing to do.

Journey into the Unknown

Chapter 2 - Trip to Venezuela

Leaving Home

In five barrels, I packed everything I thought I would need for living in the jungle for four years. I packed clothing, medicine, a camping stove, dishes, pots and pans, towels and wash clothes, silverware, a typewriter, books to read, material to make clothes, simple tools, and one fruit cake (given to me at Christmas to keep for the next Christmas). These were my supplies! It doesn't seem like much for four years, but I found out later that older missionaries felt I had packed to the extreme. On February 6, 1963, my parents drove me to New Orleans, Louisiana. My brother followed in a pick-up truck which carried my five barrels containing all my supplies. So, my journey to Venezuela began.

I boarded the ship with my five barrels and mixed feelings. I eagerly anticipated my voyage and my eventual arrival to Venezuela, and at the same time I was grieved leaving my family behind for four years. I sat and played my accordion, maybe not so good, to try to keep my mind occupied. After four days in New Orleans waiting for the cargo to

Loading Barrels on Ship

Trip to Venezuela

be loaded on the ship, we departed for Mobile, Alabama. I traveled on a Dutch cargo ship, the Delft, which had accommodations for only a few passengers. There were nine of us total. I was blessed to be able to travel with Ed and Irma Killam, an elderly couple who had been missionaries in Venezuela for many years. I was a very naïve, young, single woman traveling alone. They took me under their wing. They had been through customs and immigration many times and knew what to expect and which offices to go to. God had ensured I would be protected during my travels by sending a missionary couple that treated me like a daughter.

As we stopped at different ports, we were delayed sometimes up to three days for cargo to be loaded before we could depart again. We took advantage of the wait time to see the locale. We traveled from Mobile, to Tampa, Florida. In Tampa, we toured the city, shopped for post cards, and enjoyed the views. Then, I finally left the United States for Venezuela February 15th. This would be my last view of the U.S. for a long time.

Dutch Cargo Ship

Three days out of Tampa, we passed Cuba. I know this because we were invited to the Captain's Control Room at that point in time. He showed us an island in the distance and said it was Cuba. He then showed us a ship in the distance between the island and us. He said that the ship was Russian and they were patrolling the Cuban waters. He

Journey into the Unknown

needed to be careful to stay in international waters or there could be trouble. That was a little unsettling, but we were experiencing the Cold War at that time. We also had an U.S. warship following us while we were passing Cuba. They communicated with blinking lights to ask us where we were going. U.S. planes flew above us to get a good look. I didn't know for sure, but I guessed they were trying to determine if we were Russian.

From Tampa, it took four days to reach our next stop, Curacao, which was a beautiful place. I was fascinated by the old-world Dutch and Caribbean style architecture the buildings exhibited. There was a waterway splitting the town, like the Venice canals, only much larger. Quaint, romantic shops and buildings overlooked the sparkling blue, Dutch Caribbean. It was breathtaking for a young girl who had never been out of the U.S. We then sailed to Aruba, another beautiful island. Missionaries had already established a mission and church plants there. We were introduced to these fellow missionaries who showed us their printing press and radio station. It was encouraging to see what God had already accomplished here and inspired me as I was heading to my own mission field for the first time.

I started writing my mom every day. This was my way of dealing with my homesickness. I wrote about the ship, the water, the ports, everything. In my youthful exuberance to share my experiences with my mom, I shared some things that probably left her a little worried about me. I wrote to her about the beauty of the gulf and moon and my sunburn from sitting on the deck. I described the pale blue sky and its beauty beyond words. I inquired if she knew of the

Trip to Venezuela

Venezuelan ship that was hijacked on the same route my ship was on. I went further and asked her if she knew of another ship that was missing that was supposed to be on our route. These seemed like innocent questions then, but I look at them now and realize that I probably caused my mom and dad to pray a little harder for my safety and the safety of everyone on board after they received that letter!

The Killams kept their eyes out for the naive Barbara who was in awe of everything. At one point, when we were in Aruba, the captain invited all of us to go over to another ship because my roommate on the Delft was transferring to that ship. It was newer and prettier and more of a passenger ship. What an adventure! Once back at our ship at dusk, the first mate asked me if I wanted to see how they pulled in the ropes and signal for the ship to start. He spoke English and was with his shipmates who were preparing the ship to leave port. It was all very interesting to me as I had never seen this before. However, the other missionary couple talked to me the next day about this. They warned me to be careful of the crew as they were unsaved and drinking most of the time. They said as a young girl I was very attractive to them and needed to be aware of this type of situation. I don't know that the first mate meant any harm as he was with lots of other people. I do know that I was very trusting, and that God put that missionary couple there to help me.

Our first stop in Venezuela was Maracaibo where the first evangelical mission was established in Venezuela. There was a large evangelical church there which had its own bookstore, printing press and radio station which was highly unusual at that time. We saw these first hand. It

Journey into the Unknown

turned out, that while I was on the mission field, I would be able to receive Spanish copies of their magazine <u>La Estrella de La Mañana</u> (The Star of the Morning) which were very inspirational to me. Caracas, my final port of the voyage, was next!

When we arrived at Port La Guaira, one of the main ship entrances to Venezuela, we went through customs and received our cargo. We then had to find a trucking company that would take our cargo from this ocean port to an inland port on the Orinoco River where our cargo would be shipped to our mission base. An English-speaking church invited us to stay in an apartment while we worked with the Venezuelan Department of Immigration to obtain our permission papers. Unfortunately, all offices were closed over the weekend and closed Monday due to President Bentancourt visiting the city. We were in Caracas six days before our paperwork was processed. After this, we signed in with the American Embassy. Finally, we boarded a plane for our last stop before the Amazon jungle.

Arrival in Venezuela

Journey into the Unknown

Chapter 3 – Puerto Ayacucho

Puerto Ayacucho was the last town where we could buy food, find medical supplies, pick-up mail, use telephones, and have access to plane services before entering the jungle. The only means of transportation after this was by river, and it was a six-day river trip via a dugout canoe with an outboard motor.

Puerto Ayacucho was the "hub" for missionaries. Support staff were there to assist missionaries living in the jungles. They secured our identification cards, took care of the mail we received from home, and bought and sent us our requested supplies. The main missionary office was there, and they received our support money and kept the books. The antiquated print shop, which was used to print translated portions of the Bible, was located there. Puerto Ayacucho also had the closest medical facilities.

Print Shop

I had arrived! I was in the country where the Lord was leading me to go, but I still did not know for sure if I would be working with one of the tribes or in a support ministry. I also did not know who would work with me as it was a requirement that single people not be out on the field alone. If anything happened out on the mission field and you were alone, there would be no one to get help, no one to find you, no one to help you survive, etc. More importantly,

Puerto Ayacucho

there would be no fellowship with anyone else who spoke your language. There was no time to dwell on this, though, because as soon as the field leadership found out that I was a typist, they asked me if I would type manuscripts for different indigenous languages. To do this, I typed the translations from the missionaries' manuscripts on to stencils. Then they used the stencils to print the booklets. It turned out that my typing in my missionary training and the year as a secretary at NTM's headquarters in Wisconsin was God's preparation for my future mission work!

I realized very quickly that I did not need to know a language to type it! However, I had to do it letter by letter. Then there were the languages that had other marks that would go over the letter or under it and in many cases, both over and under. I learned that there was what we would call a 'dead key' which didn't move until you were finished with a letter that required marks over and/or under it. It had to be a special key installed on the typewriter. This became very tedious while typing on a stencil for printing. I made many mistakes and had to do many stencils over, but I learned quickly.

While I was typing manuscripts, I was told that a boat would be coming in from an upriver station (the jungles) and that there would be a letter for me from our field leadership. After the boat arrived, there was a knock at my door. A handsome, dark haired, brown-eyed young man, wearing a Khaki shirt and pants was looking for me. He introduced himself. He told me he had a letter for me from his Dad, Curt Findley. The letter asked if I would join their team working both as a typist and a missionary with the Piaroa tribe. Yes! I would!

Journey into the Unknown

Fred Findley

The reason they needed a typist was because this young man was doing the translation of the New Testament in the Piaroa language. He would translate scripture. Then he would stop and type it out (no computer in those days). After that, he gave his translation to his translator helpers to check for mistakes or question something they didn't understand. That is where I came into the picture. They asked if I would do the typing and proofreading for him, so that he could focus on translating full-time for the Piaroa tribe. Of course, they encouraged me to pray about it first.

As I considered this request, my belongings that had been shipped with me on the Dutch cargo ship had not arrived. They still had to clear customs and be trucked to where they could be shipped to me via the Orinoco River in Puerto Ayacucho. While I was waiting for my shipment to arrive, I was engulfed in typing manuscripts. During this time, I had cut stencils for 25 books in nine different indigenous languages from Venezuela and Colombia. It was also a time to start learning the Spanish language and culture, even though we did not have a Spanish course in those days for new missionaries.

Since Puerto Ayacucho was the hub of the work, I enjoyed getting to meet many of the missionaries as they passed through for various reasons. One family that I met was the

Puerto Ayacucho

Neese family. Mrs. Neese came to Puerto Ayacucho from their jungle base to give birth to their fourth child. Elna, the oldest daughter, was probably 19 years old. She came with her mother to help her with the other daughters as the father stayed in the jungle with their son. While she was there, she and I met briefly as we were both busy; she with children and her mom and me with my manuscript typing. During this time, the leadership talked with me about Elna Neese. Her parents were going home on furlough in a year, and she recently finished high school. The opportunity arose for her to go home by herself now and start Bible School or stay until her parents' furlough came up in a year. She decided she wanted to be involved in missions in a tribe for the next year and then go home with her parents after that. Since she was a single girl, and I was a single girl, leadership talked with us about working together for the next year. I had a partner!

I also met a missionary couple, Derek and Jill Hadley, who were very special to me. Derek knew "how to do things" and I had been in NTM Language training in Wisconsin with Derek and Jill, so I knew both already. When Derek and Jill arrived at Puerto Ayacucho to start their ministry, she was pregnant, and it was best that they stay there until after the baby came. They fit right in, and he was a big help in the print shop and any area he was needed. He also made some furniture for their baby as they had nothing. He made me a book case and a couple kitchen cabinets for when I moved in to a tribe. There was a sadness, though. When Jill gave birth, the baby was born breach which resulted in the baby dying. This was the first funeral that I had witnessed in a foreign country. We stood together with them in prayer and saw how the Lord sustained them. Their acceptance of

Journey into the Unknown

this was example to all of us. They never gave up! They went into the Yanomamö (Guaica) tribe and served the Lord for many years.

Since we had visitors from the States, we also had the opportunity to go to a small Piaroa village. This was my first glimpse of a Piaroa village and the large palm circular house, called a "churuata" that they all lived in together. There were no windows, and the door was only three feet high to keep wild animals out. We had to stoop down to go in, and then we had to stand still for a while until our eyes became accustomed to the darkness. The house was full of smoke as each family had their individual cooking fire and there was no means of ventilation. The reality of their living conditions was shocking. However, this was all they had known.

Inside the house each family had a pie shaped area starting next to the wall and coming out to almost the middle. As I looked around, each family had their own fire and hammocks hung around the fire. Pets were loose inside. Crawling babies had a cord tied around their ankles which was attached to a stick in the ground to keep them out of the fires. The middle section of the round house was reserved for visitors. This was supposed to be the honored place but was the least private.

We had a young Maquiritare tribal girl staying with us while she was under medical treatment in Puerto Ayacucho. She was found one day using my toothbrush to clean her shoes. She had seen some of the ladies using old toothbrushes for doing that and to her there was no difference.

Puerto Ayacucho

The single missionary ladies lived together in one of the houses on the missionary base. The privacy and protection wall that surrounded most buildings stopped at the edge of our house. So, the

Mission Complex in Puerto Ayacucho

kids in town loved to stare in our windows and watch us. We were the best TV show in town! If they couldn't see through the curtains, they would all blow on them at the same time to open them up for a fast look. They also all wanted to come in the house, but we learned quickly that was not a good idea. There always seemed to be things missing when they left.

Indian Statue

We also learned that we had free entertainment every weekend without having to leave the house. On the road where we lived, there was a roundabout with a statue in the middle and a low wall all around it. The statue was a Piaroa with a blow gun and marked the beginning of the Amazon tribal territories. This roundabout and statue were a busy place on the weekends when the town drunks gathered to drink. The more they drank the louder they talked and the louder they sang. They often came to our windows to serenade us. We didn't get a lot of sleep between them and the tropical heat.

Journey into the Unknown

Finally, after five months, my shipment of five 50-gallon barrels with all my belongings from America arrived at Puerto Ayacucho. I was ready to go upriver for my first assignment. I was ready to start my journey of serving the Lord among the Piaroas with a six-day trip up the Orinoco River.

Journey into the Unknown

Chapter 4 - Trip Upriver

The day had finally arrived, and I was on my way to the Piaroa Tribe. I was so thankful for the experiences and things I had learned while in Puerto Ayacucho in preparation for the future. A couple of the missionary ladies asked me one day if I had gotten homesick yet. They both knew my parents very well and the relationship I had with them. At that moment, I realized I hadn't even thought about being homesick since arriving in Venezuela. What an answer to prayer.

We could not leave directly from the port in Puerto Ayacucho because there were impassable rapids on the Orinoco river at that location. So, several big trucks took all the people, supplies

Leaving for Upriver

for the upriver missionaries, and our personal cargo to the port of Samariapo, 40 miles from our Mission Headquarters. Once there, the trucks were unloaded. At this port, the shore of the Orinoco was made of huge boulders. No dirt or sand was visible. They unloaded our cargo onto the boulders where it waited to be loaded on to the supply boats.

As we stood there patiently watching and swatting the gnats, we thought it would be impossible for all the cargo and passengers to fit in the one big boat even with its two smaller boats attached. Most boats were dugout canoes, but

Trip Upriver

this boat was so big that it was made from boards and measured roughly 40 feet long and 10 feet wide! On the prow of the boat, they put the 50-gallon barrels of gas and kerosene needed by the people upriver. My barrels with my belongings were put there. The Piaroas used one of my barrels to hold down the anchor in the big boat! They also fit one of the cabinets that Derek built for us. Now, Elna and I would not have to cook on the floor with our little camp stove.

Cargo for Trip

The helpers and missionaries had managed to fit everything on to the boats. They had figured out how to make the most of all the space. Since it would be a lengthy trip (5-6 days) this boat had a thatched roof to protect the passengers and cargo from the rain and the sun. Boards had been nailed to the sides and poles nailed to the boards to hold up the thatched roof.

This supply boat would be home to 15 of us for the next five or six days. For sleeping arrangements, most slept in hammocks. However, I was new to this, so I wanted to sleep on my mattress that I had brought with me. My "mattress" was a 4-inch thick piece of foam rubber covered with cloth. They put my mattress on the top of suitcases packed together, and that is where I slept. Unfortunately, the suitcases shifted with the rocking of the boat. I was so uncomfortable, more with each passing day, that the last night I decided to finally try to sleep in the hammock I had brought.

Journey into the Unknown

The boat had a very interesting bathroom…an outhouse on the back of the boat. You had to walk on the side of the boat (8 inches wide) and hold on to the thatched roof while the boat was moving to get to it. It only had three walls and a roof, and it was all made of aluminum roof sheeting.

There was a door in the front, but since there was no one behind the outhouse, the back was open. I put off going back there until I couldn't stand it any longer. I finally got up enough nerve to get up

Supply Boat

and head to the outhouse. Everyone knew what I was going to do! This was new to me, and so it was scary and embarrassing, yet at the same time a blessing! A blessing because there was an outhouse, so we didn't have to stop all the time and tie up to find a place to relieve ourselves. Thankfully, I never heard of anyone that fell in the river while occupying the outhouse.

Our "kitchen" was close to the prow of the boat and just behind the river guide's seat. It consisted of two wooden boxes on their sides. On the top was a camp stove on one side and the other side there was a place to work to prepare food. The open side of the boxes was for storage of utensils for cooking and food supplies. Our cooking was very limited. Some of the food that didn't need to be refrigerated was prepared before we left the town. We took turns cooking; two women cooked together one day and two the next day. Whenever we needed water for drinking or cooking, we would get it from the river. Dishwashing was very simple; we just held the metal plates and spoons over

Trip Upriver

the side of the boat and they got a good cleaning with the running water. The only problem with this was if you didn't have a good grasp of the dishes, they were swallowed up by the beautiful Orinoco River. We had accidentally donated to the river dishes, silverware, pressure cookers and even a camp stove that caught on fire.

Being a naïve, new missionary, some of the seasoned missionaries on board enjoyed teasing me. On the first night they thought they would play a joke on me and told me that the electricity would be going off soon. Sure enough, the sun went down, and so did our "electricity."

When it wasn't raining, and the moon was out, the river guides that were running the motors stayed up as late as they could to make better time. Even after staying up late, they would still get up early in the morning. Most of the passengers felt it was good sleeping with the drone of the motors and the fresh air in a swinging hammock. It felt good to me too as long as I was sleeping on the foam mattress not the hammock!

One night, when it started raining hard, the river guides had to pull over to the shore and tie the boats to a tree. We could hear the helpers bailing out any water that might have blown in or leaked into the boats. The smaller boats, tied to both sides of the big one, did not have roofs and they could fill up with rain or leak from holes in them. If one of them were to sink, this would cause the other boats to sink also as they were all tied to the big boat. So, bailing water was a necessity for our safety. As we were traveling along, we also found a smaller canoe floating down river. The river guides wanted to take it with us as it was in good shape. So, they just pulled it up across the front of one of the other boats and off we went!

Journey into the Unknown

I heard much about the set of rapids that we would be going through on this trip. To a first timer, this was scary. The first set of rapids were called the "rapids of death," and they were worse during the rainy season, which was the season that we were in. The water was as smooth as glass. Then we saw bubbling in the distance. The bubbling quickly turned into churning as we drew closer and grew more and more turbulent because of the large rocks just below the surface of the water. The river guides pushed the boat away from rocks with their paddles. They knew the rivers better than anyone and knew the best parts to go through. I did a lot of praying while the guides did much work.

We occupied ourselves with different things during the day while traveling. One of the ladies washed a dress using the abundant amount of running water that we had available. Since we had a baby on board and this was before the days of disposable diapers, diapers also had to be washed the same way. We had temporary clothes lines tied from one pole to another for drying the clothes. They were either made of heavy rope or bejuco, a strong vine that grows in the jungle. I stayed busy writing letters, reading books and doing my part in the cooking. Work or not, we all stayed busy looking at the jungle and taking in all the pure, untouched beauty of God's creation.

We arrived in TamaTama at 11 p.m. a day ahead of schedule. Because the jungle nights were very quiet, the missionaries woke up from the sound of the motors on the river. From the boat, we saw kerosene lights being turned on in the window of one house after another. Before long, these lights started moving down to the port to welcome us. There was a lot of excitement as the folks were glad to see

Trip Upriver

us. Of course, they also might have been excited to receive mail from home and their food and fuel supplies for the next three months!

TamaTama was the location of the missionary children's school, and it was also where the supplies were left for the missionaries living and working in different locations in the Orinoco river tributaries. We called these missionaries the "upriver missionaries." Their supplies were sent from TamaTama to them by smaller dugout canoes. Across from TamaTama was Punta Piaroa. Punta Piaroa would be the first base I would work at. I was excited to finally arrive; I had been preparing for this for the past six years.

Journey into the Unknown

Chapter 5 - Piaroa Tribe and the Findleys

The Piaroa tribe was spread over several large rivers, tributaries, and a large area of the jungle about 100 square miles. The first NTM missionaries started to work with the Piaroa tribe after Margaret Gormley and Mary Lou Yount went to San Juan de Manapiare in February 1949. There were a few Piaroas living there, and Margaret and Mary Lou started developing a written language for the Piaroa language. They would use this to teach the Piaroas to read and write and eventually to read the New Testament in their own language.

Not much was known about the Piaroas in those days. One missionary described the Piaroas as "a large group submerged in time.... exterminating each other by means of Satan's power." The Piaroas were so isolated that they thought they were the only people that existed on the earth. They had witchdoctors who would put curses on people. These witchdoctors had satanic power over the tribe. There was such a fear of the witchdoctor that their lives were guided by whatever the witchdoctor said. He was a supreme being to them as that was all they knew.

In 1950, Kathy Earle and Avonne Smith went to the Isla de Raton, "Rat Island", a small-town close to Puerto Ayacucho, to learn Spanish. There they became acquainted with a young Piaroa man, Bautista Silva, whose father had arranged for Bautista to live with a family to learn Spanish. They also met Bautista's father, Juancito, the village captain, and other relatives that visited him. Later, they visited Juancito's village and lived there for two months on

Piaroa Tribe and the Findleys

the Siapapo river. These things happened before there was a Catholic station there, and before the decree was made that anyone entering indigenous territory had to acquire written permission from the national government. When that decree was made, Robert Shaylor, our field chairman, went to Caracas to obtain the needed permission. After Avonne Smith married and went to another tribe with her husband, Kathy Earle and Mary Lou Yount returned to Juancito's village twice before they were granted temporary permits. During the second visit in 1950, Margaret Gormley joined them.

Bautista was the only man of the group who spoke Spanish. He spoke enough to help develop the written language, however, he was not open to the Gospel. If any mention of either his beliefs or ours was made, his face became an impervious mask and the discussion went no further. At the end of their stay, the missionaries left the area with saddened hearts.

It was two years later before the missionaries had further contact with any of the Piaroas. Because the government contract with the Catholic church had gone into effect, all non-Catholic missionaries had to leave all the areas the Catholic permit covered. So, they moved to San Juan. However, the Lord continued to work as He gave the NTM missionaries contact with Bautista once again. He was interested in what the missionaries were doing, so, he took his family to live with them in San Juan for five months to serve again as a language translator. During this time, Bautista and his wife learned to read in Spanish. He finally announced to them, "When I understand all about this, I too, will believe in Jesus Christ and walk with Him."

Journey into the Unknown

Juan Bautista

When Bautista left San Juan to return to his tribe, he planned to return to San Juan with his whole family. Unfortunately, the witchdoctor warned his father, Captain Juancito, that there were many evil spirits on the Ventuari River. So, Bautista's family and friends were too afraid to move up to San Juan. Eventually, the missionaries found out that Bautista had continued reading the Gospel every night. He would light his lamp and read the Gospel presentation in Spanish. He had stopped taking dope and chanting to evil spirits with the other men. Chanting was a tribal duty of every Piaroa man. Even though the missionaries had to leave Juancitos' village which was under the Catholic permit, they had heard there were NTM missionaries on the Orinoco River further up. The Piaroas wanted to learn more from the missionaries. The Lord had put a desire in their hearts to know more about the Gospel. So, Captain Juancito said to his group, "If they can't come to live with us, then let's go live with them." It took over a year to prepare for the move. At last they loaded their possessions and the food they had prepared into the canoes and started up the river to find the missionaries.

Captain Juancito

At the town of San Fernando de Atabapo, they met a Venezuelan national who knew the missionaries. He told

Piaroa Tribe and the Findleys

them where the missionaries were, but assured them they could never reach them in the canoes they were in. So, the group went up the river further and built a village called Puruname on the Orinoco River. It was there the Findleys went down to visit them in this new village and stayed with them several months. During this time Bautista, and his immediate family, accepted Christ as their Savior.

Captain Juancito eventually learned the missionaries were located at TamaTama. Since this was on the Orinoco River, and the witchdoctor hadn't told them of evil spirits on the Orinoco, he asked if missionaries could live with them and teach them if they moved nearby.

Their move from their original village took about six years as it was over 400 miles by river. They paddled upriver against the current. They took all their food and belongings. When they ran out of food, they stopped and planted a garden. Once the food was harvested, they moved upriver again. They had to repeat this every year. Finally, in 1959, they arrived at Puruname which was close to where the Findleys were located. They went to Puruname and learned more of the Piaroa language and then taught them to read and write and to learn God's Word. The Piaroas made one more move and built their new village across the river from TamaTama and called the place Punta Piaroa. What a joy it was for missionaries Curt and Allie Lee Findley to see these people turn from darkness to light and from the power of Satan to God!

The Findleys were based at TamaTama with their son, Fred, who was 15. At that young age, he was immersed into the Piaroa culture. He would later use his knowledge of the language and culture in the profession God would call him

Journey into the Unknown

The Findleys, 1954

to! Before his calling, though, he had a little fun with the Piaroas. For fun, in Fred's eyes, the entire village went to a lake with large, long poles and waded into the lake hitting the water in front of them. This would scare everything in the water away from them and onto the sandbars. Everyone made their way across the lake as waves of the larger fish and alligators fled ahead of them. Once people came close to the other side of the lake, the turtles went up on the sand bar where the women and children grabbed them and turned them over on their backs to immobilize them. The turtle was a source of food for the villagers.

Initially, the Piaroas had a hard time distinguishing the difference between Fred's name and his father's as they both had the same Spanish name. Curtis Findley was Curtis Frederick Findley and there was no Spanish word for Curtis, so they used Federico. Frederick Lee Findley was the son. So, in Spanish they were both called Federico for Frederick. The Piaroas were confused that they both had the same name. One of the missionary ladies decided to eliminate that problem. She told the people to call the father Federico and the son Perico. We didn't know why, but we assume because the names sounded similar. She did not realize that Perico was the name for a parakeet when she suggested it. Being a foreigner, she assumed that it would be short for Federico. They liked that idea so much that from that time to this very day, they refer to Fred as

Piaroa Tribe and the Findleys

Perico. Later in his life, he was called his nickname even in high government places and in several books in which he was mentioned.

Fred went to school in TamaTama as that was the school base. He used a small dugout canoe with an outboard motor to cross the river to TamaTama from Punta Piaroa. He kept a knife with him in the canoe just in case he needed it, and it was lodged in between the seat and the shell of the boat. One day he headed across river to TamaTama. When he was almost to the other side of the river, the motor stopped. As it drifted closer to the shore, it hit another boat and flipped over. Fred ended up in the water clinging to the boat. There were Piranhas in the water…man eating fish! As adventurous as Fred was, this wasn't the type of adventure he wanted. When his boat tipped over, his hand was cut by the knife he brought, and his fingers bled. The Piranha were on the look-out for blood and whatever it was flowing from. Unfortunately for the Piranha, Fred had his wits about him enough and stuck his bleeding fingers in his mouth and swam to shore unharmed.

There were several different kinds of snakes in the area. They were found in the palm walls of the houses, in the cupboards, in the dressers, and on trails walking through the jungle. One of Fred's favorite past times was finding large anaconda snakes (boa constrictors) 15 feet or more in length sleeping on the sandbar. Fred and his friends snuck behind it, tied one end of a

Boa Constrictor

Journey into the Unknown

rope around its tail and another end to the bench in a dugout canoe with an outboard motor. They then started the engine and tried to pull the snake into the water. There would be a brief struggle, until it came fully awake. They cut the rope free from the canoe and fled before the snake could sink the canoe and get revenge.

The Findley's son was also a sleepwalker! One day he was in a Piaroa house sleeping. They always kept a fire going all night and all day as they didn't have an easy way to start a fire. Therefore, someone stayed awake, in shifts, to ensure the fire was always going. One night, according to the Piaroas, Fred got up and danced around the fire screaming, "Fire ants are biting me!" "Fire ants are biting me!" The Piaroas tried to tell him everything was alright and eventually got him back in his hammock. The next morning, the people told him what he had done. His parents had warned the villagers that at times he sleepwalked, and this confirmed it. The Piaroas were a little concerned for Fred. They talked and laughed about it for a long time.

Fred eventually followed in his parents' footsteps. He attended the New Tribes Language Institute (NTLI). Because he had spent four years with the Piaroa tribe, he already spoke the language perfectly. He had done some translation with his folks in TamaTama, and he had already translated scripture verses, songs and Bible stories. So, NTLI accelerated his training program. He took specialized training in Bible translation and linguistics only. In May of 1960, he went back to TamaTama with his parents. He began translation work by helping the other missionary, Mary Lou Yount. He worked with her to form an alphabet,

Piaroa Tribe and the Findleys

to create a grammatical structure of the language, and to get the Piaroa language in to written form.

Journey into the Unknown

Chapter 6 - Punta Piaroa

In mid-1963, at Punta Piaroa, Elna and I were ready to study the language and teach literacy. The Piaroas had built a 15X30 foot room attached to Captain Juancito's house for us. The room had a thatched roof, mud walls and dirt floor just like theirs. There was an eight-foot mud wall that went almost all the way across the room with enough space for a doorway to the back. In the back was our bedroom and dressing area. The kitchen, table and benches were in the front where people could sit and visit. There were a couple windows in the front, so we often had observers looking in from the outside.

First Home in Tribe

During the day, we were always under the watchful and curious eyes of many, especially the children. They would talk as fast as they could and laugh while watching us go about cooking, typing, sewing, or anything at all. They really were fascinated over my typing; especially when I could keep typing and look at them and not at the keyboard. How I longed for the day that I could speak their language and understand what they said.

One of our major physical battles was with the gnats that bit during the day and the mosquitoes that came out at night. They especially loved to bite the new missionaries who were not used to them and had fresh blood. Their bites left little red blood spots which itched and burned. The women used a stick whittled down to a sharp point as a solution. They pricked the blood spot with the stick which

Punta Piaroa

gave us immediate relief. One time I had so many bites that I had two Piaroa girls working on me at the same time; one on each arm. I felt they enjoyed it as this was something they could do for us to show that they cared. I soon learned that despite the tropical heat, it was wise to wear long pants and long-sleeved shirts!

Washing Clothes

We washed our clothes in the river where we also took our baths. We always tried to go after the gnats went away and before the mosquitoes came out at night. We had one hour. The ladies always watched to see when we went to the river to wash clothes. They liked to go with us, because they knew we had soap for washing the clothes. They would ask if they could borrow it for washing their clothes. This was a good time to win their confidence and communicate with them using our limited knowledge of their language.

Our co-workers, Curt and Allie Lee Findley, moved in 1960 to Punta Piaroa and lived in a house across the path from us. The Findleys were very fortunate, because they had a kerosene refrigerator. They were on home assignment the year before and acquired it then. To ship it to Venezuela, they tried to use all the empty spaces in the fridge to bring things down from the U.S. One of the special treats they packed in the refrigerator was a case of peanut butter. They still had extra space, so they packed clothes around the jars of peanut butter. The clothes kept

Journey into the Unknown

the jars from breaking, but what they didn't realize was that some of their clothes had the smell of moth balls. This smell penetrated through the glass jars and changed the flavor to moth ball peanut butter. What a

Co-Workers

disappointment, but since no one wasted anything good or useful on the mission field (neither the missionaries nor the villagers), they ate it anyway. They didn't recommend the new flavor!

To us the things we brought were not much. To the Piaroas, it was an unbelievable number of things. We had a "troja", a loft, to store the three months' supply of food, medical supplies and trading goods (things the villagers wanted such as fish hooks, fish line, soap, etc.) until we needed them. Since everything had arrived in cardboard boxes, we would keep the things we needed right away down stairs and store the rest in the loft. We accessed the loft by using a ladder made by the Piaroas from small poles tied together with vines brought in from the jungle.

When we first arrived at Punta Piaroa, we had to boil our drinking water. However, after we put on tin roofs, we used fifty-gallon metal barrels (that we had brought our belongings in from the States) as a tank to catch rain water from the roof. We would cover the barrels with a clean cloth to keep things from falling into the water. We cut a small hole in the bottom of the barrel and attached a pipe with a spigot to it. We had running water!

Punta Piaroa

The joint outhouse for the missionary families in the village was different than the one on the boat. It was located a block from our house at the far end of the village right on the edge of the jungle. To get to it, we walked in front of all the Piaroa houses. They always asked us where we were going and laughed at us as the villagers did not have outhouses; they had paths into the jungle that served their needs.

We appreciated our little outhouse which the Piaroas teased us about. One day, we were told that tigers had come into the village, and they attacked one of the hogs that ran loose. So, the villagers went out with their shotguns and came back with a big tiger. Everyone thought the danger had passed. The relief did not last long, though, as it turned out the tiger was a female and that meant that there was an angry male out there looking for his mate. It was a scary trip to the outhouse from then on!

The river was another adventure all its own. Another missionary loaned us a 5 1/2 horse power outboard motor. I didn't know how to operate one, but Elna had a lot of experience as a MK (missionary kid). The motor was big enough for us to go back and forth from Punta Piaroa to TamaTama, but not so powerful that we couldn't handle it.

One evening we were invited across the river to TamaTama to have a meal with one of the missionary families living there. We were having such a good time that we didn't realize how dark it was getting. When the sun went down in the jungles, it went down fast. It was dark when we started back to Punta Piaroa, and we had just one flashlight. I was scared crossing the river at night but didn't want to say anything as I didn't want to appear cowardly. We got in the

Journey into the Unknown

boat and pushed out from the river bank before we started the motor. We soon realized this was a bad idea as, for the first time since we received it, the motor would not start. Elna pulled and pulled on it. As she tried to start it, the boat started floating down the fast-moving waters of the Orinoco river (and we needed to go across not down). We started paddling towards the shore, but soon we were out of sight. Fortunately, the missionaries at TamaTama realized they had not heard the motor start and became concerned. They started looking for us.

We finally got the motor going, and we started upriver again. By that time, however, there were lights coming down the hill from TamaTama which indicated people were looking for us. This was a relief as the motor worked for a while but stopped again. Two of the men came to our rescue and towed the boat with us in it back to Punta Piaroa. From this experience, and many more, we learned that God was always watching over us and protecting us in spite of our inexperience and lack of wisdom.

When the villagers heard what had happened on the boat, they asked about the "light" I had with me…the flashlight. They heard that it would float in the water and glowed in the dark. They could not believe it, so they wanted to see it work. They took it out in the dark and tried it out. Then another group of Piaroas, after hearing about the flashlight, wanted to try it out. So, in the end, my flashlight gave them something to laugh about and made the rest of the village laugh as the word about the mysterious flashlight spread. It seems it was very easy for us to become their entertainment!

Punta Piaroa

There were a lot of firsts for me in those early days, also. Besides the river, the gnats, and the outhouse, we were starting to learn the Piaroa culture and their language. Once we learned some of the language, we started classes with the children in the morning while their parents were out planting their gardens. We taught them to read, write, and basic math skills. The men were often away making canoes from the trees that they cut down in the jungles. After they returned, we held classes with the adults in the evening. Any free time Elna and I had, we continued to study the language.

Most of the Piaroas had never seen their language in writing; all they knew was what they could speak. It was new to them to read their own language and to learn how to write it on paper. We taught them to read using basic phonics and then to practice reading using simple Bible stories. These stories had been translated by Fred Findley. All of this was in preparation for giving them the Word of God in their own language which was currently in the early stages of the tedious process of translation.

One day the Findleys approached Elna and me about making a trip with them, the Killam family, and a Piaroa family to San Juan where their son, Fred, was working with the Piaroas. They wanted to check on him as he had moved to San Juan to start a ministry and continue translation. San Juan was a centrally located Piaroa village on the Manapiare River. The first missionaries working with the Piaroas arrived in this area in 1949. Curt and Allie Lee started working there in the late 1950's for a period before moving on to another area. This was my first trip to San Juan.

Journey into the Unknown

We went in the Findley's family boat which was about 40 feet long with a tin roof. This was a smaller boat than the one I had first traveled on up the well-known Orinoco River to TamaTama! Also, unlike my initial trip upriver, this trip only took four days and that was a good thing as there was not enough room for us to sleep on this boat. To sleep, our guide found small villages with people still in them, or even abandoned villages if necessary where we could hang our hammocks to spend the night. This worked the first two nights.

Our third night traveling, the guide found an abandoned house with no walls and a palm roof. We hung our hammocks and slept a couple hours until it started raining. Then we realized the roof had a lot of holes in it. We had to pack up our hammocks and mosquito nets and move back to the boat for the rest of the night. In the boat, we had to sit up, but at least we had a roof. The last night we couldn't find an abandoned house or cleared off space to tie our hammocks. The farther we went upriver, the denser the jungle became.

It was getting late, and the guide finally had to stop. He found a big tree to tie the boat to for the night. We had to climb a bank so steep it took two men to help us up. They had to cut away the smaller trees to clear out a place to hang the hammocks. Elna and I did just fine hanging our own hammocks and mosquito nets. I was feeling better about the whole situation until the more experienced missionaries told us why they all tried to hang their hammocks in a circle around the fire and kept a fire going all night. They used this set up with the hopes that if a tiger came around looking for food, they would either be afraid

Punta Piaroa

of the fire or eat the dog we had brought rather than eating us!

All through the night, I kept hearing strange sounds in the jungle. I was sure glad that the other nights we had a place to sleep even if it was a cleared off place with an abandoned house and a leaking roof. I was reminded again that God was with us where ever we were; whether that was in the jungles or in what seemed to be a safe place.

After three and a half days on the river, we arrived at San Juan. I stepped foot off the boat at San Juan. Unbeknownst to me, I was stepping into the world that eventually would become my home for the next 25 years.

Even though we were there a short time for this visit, we had the opportunity to get to know the people and visit several different villages in the surrounding areas. When we returned to Punta Piaroa, Curt stayed in San Juan with the Piaroa couple from Punta Piaroa that had gone with us and his son returned with us to Punta Piaroa to work on translation with Bautista.

Shortly after Elna and I returned to Punta Piaroa, we were approached by Piaroas about taking a trip with them to a new area in the jungle. They needed a place to plant their gardens as they didn't plant gardens in their village. Most of the Piaroas would move up to the head of a small river to spend time planting a new garden called a "conuco." They would be gone a month. We were in the middle of teaching them when this occurred, and we wondered how this would work. Fortunately, the villagers did not want to miss out on classes. They asked if Elna and I could stay with them to

Journey into the Unknown

continue teaching them reading and writing. We agreed! God always has a plan!

First, the villagers went ahead and built houses and prepared for the garden. As all the tribal people lived in one house, they offered to build Elna and me a small house of all palm leaves with a small opening for a door to keep the wild animals out while we were upriver with them. They knew, and accepted, that we were different and were very accommodating to prepare this for us ahead of time. They even weaved a palm mat as a door to cover the opening. They were so glad to have us that they weaved more mats to put under our hammocks and to sit on. They also made us several benches from small trees to put our camp stove on and our suitcases. It is amazing how God works. We were there to serve them, but they were serving us in big ways also!

Villagers' House at Garden

We had endured diseases and the jungle; now we would experience more of the dangers of the river as we went upstream. The caño is a small creek and there were a lot of rocks and fallen trees that we had to maneuver. In some cases, we had to get out of the boat, unload the cargo and stand on the tree in the river while the Piaroas pushed the boat over or under the tree. Then we reloaded the cargo, got back in, and proceeded upstream.

While we were upriver for the planting of their gardens, we received a letter from Allie Lee Findley that her husband,

Punta Piaroa

Curt, had arrived from San Juan deathly sick with malaria. She asked us to return as she was alone in the village. Fred, her son, was off in another location translating with Bautista, and she had sent a letter for him to come back also. The villagers, that brought the letter to us, took Elna and I downstream in a canoe to be with Allie Lee. They paddled for five hours to get us down to the Findley's house. The Piaroa couple that was staying with Curt in San Juan brought him via open canoe to Punta Piaroa, a four to five-day trip. They never thought he would arrive alive, but he did although he was in a coma. There was a lot of prayer for him by both missionaries and the Piaroas. We thanked the Lord for answered prayer as we saw him getting better each day. When we knew he was out of danger, we returned to the upriver village and remained there until they finished planting their gardens. We thanked God again for answered prayer

The time had come for Elna to leave for the U.S. with her parents. The big question was what do I do and where do I go now, since I no longer had a partner? Did I stay in the village alone? I was sure both Cecil Neese (Elna's father) and Fred's Dad, Curt, both being members of the field leadership, were concerned about my being alone and discussed it with the rest of the leadership team. Since the Findleys were holding down two bases, San Juan and Punta Piaroa, they decided to return to San Juan as a family. They asked me if I would move there with them and help their son with his translation work. It was finally time to help with translation typing! There were other areas there that I could minister in also such as teaching the adults and children to read, medical care, dental care and whatever

Journey into the Unknown

else was needed. This was God's way of leading me into the next step of my life.

"As for God, His ways are perfect." Psalm 18:30

Journey into the Unknown

Chapter 7 - The "Ringing of the Bells"

I made my second long boat trip to San Juan. This time, though, it was not for a visit but to work with the Piaroas in any capacity needed which included typing the translation of the New Testament.

River Travel

The first project I was assigned was typing the manuscript of Acts that Fred had recently translated into the Piaroa language. I had already typed many different languages, but the Piaroa language was the hardest to type as it had so many variations (a, ä, a̱, etc.) for the same letter. I was glad for the experience I had in Puerto Ayacucho typing tribal manuscripts a few years before.

The indigenous people in the San Juan area did not have access to a dentist. Many of them suffered from multiple cavities and tooth decay. Before our dental assistance, their way of taking care of a toothache was severe. They took a sharp pointed stick and placed it against the tooth that hurt. Then they hit that stick with another stick to break the tooth off. Unfortunately, this did not take care of the pain but rather added to the problem as infections would then set in. Many times, they had to have an antibiotic treatment before we could do any procedure. Besides being a typist, I had now become a "dental assistant!"

The "Ringing of the Bells"

Fred Pulling Teeth

Fred had been in the States and asked a dentist friend if he could observe how to pull teeth as he knew the Piaroas needed this procedure. After observing the dentist for an extended time, Fred procured the necessary hand equipment to pull teeth in Venezuela. Extractions became Fred's Saturday morning ministry as people would line up to have their hurting teeth pulled. Piaroas would come down from upriver villages for "dental services." Fred's "dental office" was a lawn chair set up outside in the middle of whatever village he was visiting. Since he had managed to talk me into being his assistant, I kept the dental tools ready for him and assisted however I could. At any village, whenever the villagers found out that Fred was leaving, they filled the house to wait in line to have their teeth pulled.

As we worked together on different projects we made a deal that he would teach me the language while I typed his manuscripts. Then things began to change. Fred would later call it the "bells started ringing." Language classes slowed down as Fred and I fell head over heels in love. Later, I recalled a former boyfriend had said to me when we broke up: "Maybe God has someone waiting for you in Venezuela." How true it was!

Journey into the Unknown

Dating on the mission field was very different from dating in the States. Fred and I loved each other, but we had to be so careful. The indigenous culture and way of thinking was so different than our own. We could not show any affection in public and dating was out of the question. The villagers were always watching everything we did, and it was easy to accidentally make cultural blunders, especially as a new missionary. So, extreme caution was necessary as we didn't want to cause any accidental misunderstandings or offenses.

For example, I slept in another house separate from the Findleys. However, we innocently found ourselves in a questionable situation. I did not have a bed to bring upriver with me, and I did not sleep very well in the hammock I had brought. On the other hand, at his house, Fred preferred a hammock. So, his parents loaned me the bed Fred was not using. When the Piaroas came to my one room house, they would ask whose bed was there, and I would innocently say it was Fred's bed. Then they asked whose hammock it was, and I said it was mine because it was! I used the hammock to sit in or take a nap (siesta) during the day. Without realizing it, this little conversation about Fred's bed and my hammock gave them the idea that we lived together. How easy it was to accidentally find myself in hard to explain situations when living among people of a different culture!

As a newly "in-love" couple, we were never alone. We were around villagers or other missionaries all the time. After the Piaroas went to bed, we took advantage of the opportunity to have some private conversations. I ate all my meals with Fred and his parents at their house, so there was no privacy there either. After a little time, we stole time

The "Ringing of the Bells"

together by doing dishes. Usually Allie Lee and I did dishes, but once Fred and I showed interest in each other, Fred would tell his Mother to go in the living room and rest or visit with the Piaroas. Then he would help me by drying the dishes. I was sure Fred thought he was very clever by offering to "help," but I was also sure his parents were sharing a knowing smile in the other room! Their son did not usually offer to help with the dishes! When the dishes were done, I would hang up the towel in a little storage room off the kitchen. Eventually, this could not be done by me alone; Fred needed to help me. In the privacy of the storage room, as we hung up the towel to dry, we would steal a kiss! That was our private, alone time at the Findleys!

Our time at San Juan quickly came to an end, and we returned to Punta Piaroa. The Findleys were preparing for home assignment. My parents, Horace and Elsie Wilson, made plans for a trip to Venezuela to see me and to visit some other tribes. The Findleys blessed me dearly by picking up my parents with their boat and taking all of us to visit the different Piaroa tribes. One day, the four of them crossed the river to visit TamaTama, and Fred and I found ourselves alone for a short time in his parent's house. We were sitting together, talking and enjoying each other's company. Then Fred turned to me and asked, "If it is the Lord's will, will you marry me?" I knew it was the Lord's will! I ecstatically said, "Yes!" What joy! We embraced and kissed. I was so happy that Fred and I had a future.

Eventually, we went over to the other side of the river and told both of our parents that we were going to marry! My parents were ecstatic but not surprised, as my mother had

Journey into the Unknown

been praying for me to meet the guy who had written the magazine article she read years before. The Findleys were excited also, their master plan had worked perfectly. Our engagement was the answer to many prayers…and not just ours!

From that point, everything happened quickly. For quite a while, I had a severe pain in my right side which we thought might be appendicitis. The field leadership recommended I return home with my parents for possible surgery the same time the Findleys were going back to the United States for furlough. Knowing both families would be in the home together, we decided to get married in the States.

Even though we were to wed, we had yet to have a first real date. For our first date, Fred had asked me if I wanted to go for a drive. We drove around in a 1959 Chevy Impala with a big emblem on the front. We took a drive along the winding country roads until Fred pulled over to the side of the road. After catching up on our hugs and kisses, he asked me a second time if I would marry him. When I again said "yes," he gave me an engagement ring! What a first date! I received my engagement ring, set a wedding date, and for a shower gift, I received an appendectomy ten days later! God has a sense of humor!

After the hugging, kissing, and appendectomy, we were married on August 15, 1964 at Grace Gospel Church in Huntington, West Virginia; the same church that my

The "Ringing of the Bells"

parents helped to start and that I grew up in. God's plans are so much bigger than ours!

The rest of our time in the States was spent visiting supporting churches and trying to raise more funds for our ministry in Venezuela. It was also a time for me to get to know the Findley family. I had a small family, but I had married into a large family. Since we both went to the field single, we each had our existing supporting churches and individuals. This was an opportunity to visit them all, introducing ourselves as a couple and sharing our goals of serving the Lord together on the mission field.

Newlyweds

I was no longer alone. I was no longer a single person on the mission field all by myself! I had a husband by my side. A friend. God was always with me, but how I appreciated the gift of a companion He had given me.

Journey into the Unknown

Chapter 8 - Returning to San Juan as a Family

In the early part of 1965, I returned to Venezuela with a husband of one year and a new family member on the way! Our field chairman, Bob Shaylor, met us at the airport, and we talked with him about how we should minister as a family. We decided that we would move to San Juan on the Manapiare River. We traveled over 700 miles on three different rivers over nine days in high water season to get to San Juan. What a first assignment as a couple!

Once we arrived at San Juan, we were encouraged to find that Ron and Dottie Conklin had already moved there ahead of us. It was a relief to have another family in San Juan to share the responsibilities. Since we had help, we branched out and visited other Piaroa villages. In this and every village, we taught literacy and shared the Word of God. We hoped these visits would grow into a church plant. At the same time, we started building a home in San Juan that would serve as our headquarters.

Initially, we lived in Fred's parents' home while building ours. They were still on home assignment, so we had the house to ourselves! The Piaroas worked on our new home and Fred oversaw the process. To build the house, trees were cut in the jungle and trimmed to make poles. Holes were dug, and the poles were put in the ground to build the frame. Small trees, about an inch in diameter, were trimmed and then cut and tied on both sides of the upright poles in the ground. On this frame, they tightly packed mud mixed with chopped grass in and around the poles to create walls. After the mud dried, they put a thinner mixture of

Returning to San Juan as a Family

mud and sand over it which served as a plaster. For the roof, rather than using palm leaves which would have to be

Finished House

Building of House

replaced every few years, we brought asbestos roofing from Puerto Ayacucho, so that we would never have to replace it. We finished the floor by leveling the dirt, dampening it with water, and then tamping it down with a block of wood nailed to a pole.

Once we moved in, we only had water from the river or rain draining off the roof. So, we always tried to conserve water. As we lived with a dirt floor, I could never sweep up all the dirt! The best I could do was settle the dust by sprinkling water left over from rinsing dishes. Over time, with the jungle heat, these floors became almost as hard as concrete. This was the first house we called home.

Journey into the Unknown

While in San Juan, I taught daily literacy classes to the women and children while Fred taught Bible classes to the men. Fred also made time to continue translating the New Testament into the Piaroa language. When other villages heard about our teaching and God's Word, they requested we go to their village to share the Gospel with them. As we visited villages, we also kept in mind that we needed to find land that we could clear for a small airplane landing strip. We heard that the Missionary Aviation Fellowship (MAF) would soon be available to us, so we needed just the right spot. We found ourselves overloaded many times, but the voice of others asking us to share the Gospel with them gave us the strength we needed.

Fred Teaching

There were many medical needs among the people where we lived. They came to our house asking for help. Though we could treat minor problems with medical supplies we already had, we were thankful there was a doctor or nurse available around the bend of the river at the Catholic mission. Since the Piaroas could not speak Spanish nor explain their medical problems to the doctor, we still had to go with them or write a note.

Fred Giving Medicine

Returning to San Juan as a Family

The doctor would send medicine with instructions back to us to explain to the Piaroas. It wasn't uncommon for us to go to the patients' houses and give them the correct dosage as they did not understand the importance of taking the right amount at the right time. On several occasions we spent long days with them not knowing if they were going to live or die. I felt so helpless as I didn't speak the language well enough yet to give them the hope of Heaven.

Another hat that we wore was naming children. It was interesting to note that when a new missionary arrived, or a new member of a missionary family was born, many newborn Piaroa babies would be named the same first name. The Piaroas gave full names pertaining to their tribal culture. So, a person's child was known as a first name plus the phrase "his father's son" or "her father's daughter." When civilization moved in, this presented a problem with medical records, school records, and identification papers. Birthdays were also a problem because they did not know a person's year or month of birth. We taught a class about the importance of times and names. We were often called on to give people names in Spanish and calculate approximate birthdays for them.

National traders would come upriver to the villages to buy food, boats, and other products from them that they then resold. Since the Piaroas didn't know the value of money, they often were cheated in these transactions. Upon their request, one of the things we tried to teach them after learning to read was the value of money, the value of each coin or bill, and the value of what they were selling. This did not always make us very popular with the traders!

Journey into the Unknown

There was another tribe, the Guajibo, originally from Colombia that lived 30 minutes downriver from us. Some of them had heard the Gospel and had accepted the Lord as their Savior, but like most of the other tribes, they had no one to teach them. They spoke a completely different language. When they heard there were missionaries upriver from them, they asked for someone to come and teach them. Some of the Guajibo men could speak Spanish and were able to translate. We went to their village once a month to provide teaching. This certainly wasn't enough, but it was what we could do at that time.

While teaching, translating, doctoring, reaching out to other villages, and naming parents and children, time flew. I was quickly in my 7th month of pregnancy when I realized I was having some problems. There was no doctor in San Juan, only a nurse. There was never a good time to leave, even for a short while, but we did not know if my problem was serious. So, we decided that we should go out of the jungle to Puerto Ayacucho to be near medical help when giving birth. To communicate with the outside world, a co-worker carried a letter downriver four or five days to MAF pilot, Don Roberson, to come. Fortunately, the villagers had already cleared a landing strip near us at San Juan.

When the plane arrived to pick us up, Fred and the pilot had enough time to check on the progress of another new airstrip in Caño Santo. When they buzzed the airstrip, they saw that the Piaroas had done a great job working on it and the pilot was able to land the plane. Fred paid the workers and talked with them about missionaries going to their villages to live and teach.

Returning to San Juan as a Family

We finally arrived in Puerto Ayacucho and stayed at the mission house. As we waited for the arrival of our baby, Fred kept busy helping the missionaries at the mission base. He also bought some lumber and built several pieces of furniture for us one of which was a bed frame for our mattress. On the mission field, most of our furniture was handmade and every piece was very special. I was thankful for a husband who could do so many different things.

Our daughter, Melanie Dawn, was born on September 3, 1965. It was a special blessing for me to have my mother and a good friend fly down and be there for her birth. Melanie was the talk of the hospital. Everyone wanted to see the little gringa (white) baby and fuss over her. We brought some cloth diapers, plastic diaper covers, a dress and booties to the hospital. The nurses asked to dress her before we left. When we arrived at the mission house, I realized that a diaper had not been used. Instead the nurses had used the plastic outer covering as the diaper!

Melanie as a Newborn

The doctor wanted us to stay in Puerto Ayacucho a month before going back to make sure Melanie was developing normally and to start her vaccinations. While there, our equipment that was shipped seven months earlier from the States finally arrived in Puerto Ayacucho. God's timing is always perfect, as Fred and several of the Piaroas, were able to leave early by river with our new equipment and belongings. He would be home before our daughter and

Journey into the Unknown

me. We were so thankful that we now had plane service. Melanie was the first newborn baby to fly on the MAF plane.

When we landed, many Piaroas were waiting with Fred for us. They all wanted to see and hold the new baby. From then on, when we went to new villages, the fears that they had about our wanting to be with them were lessened when they saw that we brought our baby with us. With Melanie, cultural barriers were broken down and hearts were opened. The villagers readily accepted us and the message that God had sent us to take to them.

Melanie was three months old when we made our first extended trip as a family of three to the village of Guayavalito. It took us four hours in an open canoe from our home in San Juan. Since we had no place of our own to stay, we moved into the round, communal house with the rest of the village. We had a little pie-shaped space without partitions. We took a fold-up play pen where we could keep Melanie most of the time. I was sure the Piaroas thought this was strange, as they would have put her on the dirt floor with a cord around her ankle attached to a stake. This is the same floor on which dogs and animals walked and did their business and upon which people spat. The common cold was one of the most frequent sicknesses among these people and they continually coughed and spat on the floor. It was a challenge with a baby in this set-up. She enjoyed throwing things out of her crib and watching the kids scramble to pick them up and give them right back to her. This was often hard for me to watch, and many things went through my mind as her toys hit the dirt floor.

Returning to San Juan as a Family

Most of the time, Melanie came through it without any serious problems. We trusted the Lord for her protection.

As this was an extended stay, we also talked with them about making a small mud house for ourselves. We and the Piaroa leaders decided to build a house that served a double purpose. Half of it we used as a living place, and the other half we used as a church/school room. We began teaching, and the villagers were overwhelmingly interested. Since we were away from our home base, we took only what we needed: food, clothing and fuel. While Fred taught the men, I would go to the river to bathe and wash clothes. The women watched for me, and when I left the house with Melanie they would follow behind. I thought they followed me because I was interesting to them. I eventually realized they loved using the blue bar soap that I had for washing clothes. Whether they wanted soap or to talk to me, this activity gave me the opportunity to speak with the women and practice using their language. We formed a bond.

The Piaroas were very curious about the outside world. A national farmer that lived downriver came to the village one day. The villagers knew of him and some had even worked for him. He arrived with a shotgun and went straight to our house. He was very upset with Fred, because he was teaching the people the value of money and work. The farmer felt we were keeping him from getting more out of the people because of our teaching. When the Piaroas saw what the farmer was doing, they quickly surrounded Fred in order to protect him. The man had no choice but to go back to his home, and he never troubled us again. God reminded us yet gain of His faithfulness and protection.

Journey into the Unknown

Chapter 9 - Plane Crash - Tragedy Hits

In September of 1967, the Venezuelan government started a program called the Cooperative Service of Public Health. They trained key villagers to become teachers and nurses in their villages. The biggest problem with this program was that the villagers did not speak Spanish like the government teachers. Fred was asked to take the course with the Piaroas and translate for them. For Fred to do this, we temporarily moved back to Puerto Ayacucho. Because of this program, Fred received a certified diploma and the new nurses went back to their villages with medical supplies and some medicine. This took a lot of the pressure off the missionaries on the bases where medical help was in short supply.

It was while we were at training that tragedy hit our family. On October 5th our MAF pilot, Don Roberson, made a trip to San Juan to take doctors there overnight. Since it was Don's birthday, he wanted to return home to Puerto Ayacucho to be with his family. He invited Fred's dad, Curt, to accompany him. Curt could spend the evening with us and his

Curt with Pilot

granddaughter as well as pick up supplies and then return

Plane Crash - Tragedy Hits

home the next day with Don. We had a great night with him, and he spoiled his granddaughter as much as he could in the few hours he was there. As planned, he left the next morning to return to San Juan.

Curt and Don Roberson took off from the airport at 11:10 a.m. Don radioed his wife, Marilyn, and Allie Lee to let them know that they were on their way and everything was fine. Don always radioed his wife every 20 minutes, gave her his location and checked on the weather ahead. When Don missed the first check-in, no one was worried because the radio went out frequently and fixing it took some time. Expecting the airplane to be landing soon, Fred's mother, Allie Lee, sent men to the airstrip (about 20 minutes downriver from San Juan) to meet them. When the plane was 15 minutes overdue, Allie Lee radioed Puerto Ayacucho to ask if Marilyn had heard from them. She had not. They waited a little longer thinking maybe Curt and Don had landed at another airstrip west of San Juan. When they were sure the plane was overdue and the radio was still silent, they sent word to the San Juan National Guard. They called Caracas for help to search for the plane as they assumed at this point it had crashed.

Meanwhile in Puerto Ayacucho, Don Bodin, mission administrator, and Señor Lanza, supervisor of the Health Department, began to alert the officials, government offices, national guards, and the local radio station to send out pleas for search planes. They were promised five planes the following morning from Caracas and San Fernando de Apure.

Not wanting to wait until the next day, they continued to request search planes. By 2:30 p.m., one commercial

Journey into the Unknown

airplane and one helicopter were flying over the route the M.A.F plane had taken. The pilots checked all the places where Don and Curt could have made an emergency landing. Fred and a fellow missionary also went on the commercial flight but saw nothing. In San Juan, Allie Lee sent five men to the Caño Santo airstrip by river just in case Don and Fred's dad had made it that far. The five men arrived the next morning but found they weren't there. Meanwhile, Allie Lee, who was still in San Juan, remained in continual radio contact with us in Puerto Ayacucho.

The following day Fred and the helicopter pilot flew over Piaroa villages located in the jungles where they could possibly land. They asked the villagers if they had heard the plane or had any information that would help. At one point during the search, they decided to land in the village of Gavilan, about 20 minutes from Puerto Ayacucho. Based on the timing of Don's one and only radio transmission, they thought this could have been a likely area to search. These villagers said they heard a small plane go over. They didn't see it, though. The villagers said they then heard what sounded like a plane turn around and head back. So, a search team was sent to that area by foot, but they found nothing.

By this time, the American Embassy from Caracas had flown in aviation fuel and offered two U.S. airplanes. The Venezuelan government also provided a helicopter and another large airplane for the search. MAF (Missionary Aviation Fellowship) sent in five planes and pilots from British Guyana, Brazil and Surinam. Several groups of Piaroas searched by foot through the mountainous area that the plane should have flown. Missionaries from our

Plane Crash - Tragedy Hits

mission and another mission came to help in the search also. All our mission stations and all the missionaries in the area were on standby on their radios to pass on any information that was radioed in. Everyone was praying as news was passed on about the missing plane from person to person.

We were overwhelmed with the care others were showing us. The governor sent word to the mission office for the women to make a list of groceries and anything else they needed to take care of the people there and those that came in for the search. He insisted that it be the very best food. There were 20 men from the outside that came to help, so the ladies fed them at the mission house and the governor furnished all the food. He had some of them sleep in his own house and found houses for others. We were blessed to have this many people, including the governor, care for all of us.

During the five days of searching, everyone wanted to help. As we received any information, we passed it on to the pilots and they checked out every area mentioned. Every time it turned out to be false. One afternoon, I took a break from the radio and went to visit one of my close friends and co-worker, Jeanne Bodin, who lived about a block away. While there, two men from town came to tell us the "good news." They told us someone had reportedly seen a pilot and passenger walking back to Puerto Ayacucho with their clothes torn and covered with blood. We immediately sent this information to the organizers of the search. They sent a team out where the men were seen, but it ended up being the last false sighting that we would receive during the search.

Journey into the Unknown

Crash Site

On Wednesday, Don Bodin arrived at the mission office with news that a M.A.F. pilot had reported scorched trees and a white wing tip reflecting through the trees just outside of Gavilan (the same area they searched on the first day). People were sent in by land to inspect the wreckage. Unfortunately, they discovered there were no survivors. They told Don who then notified Fred. As heartbreaking as the news was, Fred had so many responsibilities that he had no time to grieve. Don did not want Marilyn and Allie Lee to hear this report over the radio. So, Don notified Marilyn in person. Fred bravely radioed Allie Lee to meet him at the airport in San Juan. Fred told her the sad news in person. He and Don flew her to Puerto Ayacucho to be with family.

The following day, the search party cleared a site close to the wreckage for the helicopter to land to remove the bodies. From all the evidence, everyone felt it was an instant death for both

Search Helicopter

Plane Crash - Tragedy Hits

Don and Curt. It appeared the plane exploded, and the bodies were thrown from it.

The governor had taken over at this point and had the caskets ready at the airport for transporting back to Puerto Ayacucho. He made available to us cars at no cost for everybody coming in for the funerals. In those days, the only vehicle NTM had was a medium-sized truck for hauling people and supplies around. The governor had even come to the mission house to greet Allie Lee, express his condolences, and make further plans for the funeral.

We saw God's hand working all the time. Even though we were grieving, we knew

> *"...that all things work together for good to them that Love God, to them who are called according to his purpose." Romans 8:28*

The believers from local churches stayed with us all night after the caskets were brought in to one of the mission houses. They supplied everyone with hot chocolate, coffee and cookies. Townspeople came in all hours of the day and night to show their respect and care.

Fred and Don Bodin at Graves

The following day the caskets were placed on the back of a truck covered with flowers for the ride to the little Venezuelan chapel. The building was

Journey into the Unknown

overflowing with townspeople and missionaries. Since the bodies had been in the jungle five days in tropical heat and they had not been embalmed, the caskets were left on the

back of the truck. After the service, families and mourners followed behind the truck to the cemetery. After a graveside prayer, the pastor introduced the governor who spoke words of deep appreciation on behalf of the Venezuelans for the lives and work of Don Roberson and Curt Findley there in the "Amazonas." One of the Venezuelan doctors that taught the medical course that Fred was taking, put his arm around him and thanked him for allowing his Dad to be buried there.

As the tropical sun intensified, we walked away from the graveside with assurance in our hearts that Don and Curt had already been a week in heaven with the Lord rejoicing in the glories of heaven and in the blessed release from these vessels of clay which had just been so tenderly laid away. The graves were side by side with each one having its individual headstones. Each had a Bible verse on it. Curt's verse was:

"For if we believe that Jesus died and rose again, even so them also which sleep in Jesus will God bring with him." I Thessalonians 4:14. For the pilot, Don Roberson, it was: "For God so loved the world, that he gave his only begotten Son, that whosoever believeth in him should not perish, but have everlasting life." John 3:16.

These stones are still there today. They stand as a witness to the Venezuelan people of God's love for them; the reason Don and Curt gave their lives.

Plane Crash - Tragedy Hits

We found out later how God had protected in miraculous ways those who were searching for the plane. Fred, with the helicopter pilot, had landed in several Piaroa villages. In most of them, there was evidence that people were there, but none were seen. Due to fear of the helicopter, they had fled into the jungles and hidden. We were told later that in one of the villages that appeared recently abandoned, the people were watching from behind trees. They had their bows and arrows pointed at Fred and the pilot and their plan was to kill them, destroy the helicopter, and burn the village down so no evidence would be left behind.

In another village, the Piaroas pointed to an area where they had heard a noise and thought the plane might have gone down. The strange thing was that they would not go with the search party to show them; they just pointed to the area. It turned out that was the place where the plane went down. We eventually found out why they wouldn't go with the search team. Shortly after the funerals, they came out to Puerto Ayacucho and gave Fred his Dad's wallet and wrist watch. They admitted that they had been to the crashed plane at the beginning of the search and had stolen some things. They were afraid that they would get in trouble if they told us earlier, so they remained silent as we searched for five days.

The news about the crash and Don and Curt continued to spread long after they were laid to rest. We received letters and cards from back home that encouraged and assured us of their prayers. In one card, a poem was sent entitled: "In Acceptance lies Peace" by Amy Carmichael. This blessed us greatly as we claimed that peace and moved forward and faced whatever God allowed in our lives and ministry.

Journey into the Unknown

Don Roberson and Family

Curt and Allie Findley

"Precious in the sight of the Lord is the death of his saints." Psalm 116:15

Journey into the Unknown

Chapter 10 – Death Brings Life

The Piaroas and indigenous believers from many tribes were deeply moved by the loss of both Don and Curt. They reacted in different ways after receiving the news. In a Yanomamo village, a witchdoctor stormed angrily when he heard of the loss (as is their custom when someone dies). The missionary talked with him at length about the situation. The witchdoctor decided that he too wanted to receive the Lord and be ready when his turn came to meet the Lord in person.

The Piaroas, however, were the ones most deeply affected by the crash. We had seen many of them become indifferent to the Gospel. We were worried about this, but Curt and Don's deaths changed that. As the months passed, the Piaroas expressed a desire to accept Christ as their savior. They explained that before the crash they were "told" about God and how to live as believers. After the crash, they "saw" how we lived out our faith and now they wanted to believe.

Later, as we reflected on the evening before Curt's last flight, we remembered he had expressed deep concern for the inroads Satan seemed to be making among the Piaroas because of a lack of personnel. Curt had commented that the Lord knew what was needed to stir people to carry on the work that still needed to be done. He said God would raise up laborers for the unreached Piaroas in the mountain areas around San Juan, the Cuao River, Caño Santo, and Caño Marieta. Seventy percent of these areas were in government restricted regions in which missionaries were not allowed to go. We were amazed at God's handiwork,

Death Brings Life

when we realized that Curt and Don had crashed and died just inside the edge of one of these restricted mountains. News of Curt's death spread through the tribe as Christian Piaroas were talking about Curt, his death, and his God. To our surprise, many villagers from the restricted areas walked for days through jungles, rivers, and over mountains to hear more about Curt and his God; a God they had heard they did not need to fear.

Fear was a way of life for the Piaroas. Their greatest fears were witchcraft and witchdoctors. Their fears were so great, that it could bring on death. Fred knew a young fellow who came from the mountains, a restricted area, to San Juan to visit his aunt. His father-in-law, a witchdoctor, told him that if he wasn't back in three months, he would put a spell on him and kill him. While he was there, he began making money to buy things and take back to his family. Time passed, and it began raining and flooded out the rivers making it impossible for him to return home. Not long after that, he said that he was going to die that day; that his father-in-law had put a spell on him for not returning in three months.

After he told Fred he was going to die, he went back to his aunt's house and lay down in his hammock. Within an hour, the aunt called because her nephew was dying. When Fred got there, he questioned the young fellow. He asked him where he was sick; what was hurting him. The young man said he was not sick but that his father-in-law had put a spell on him and that he was dying. While Fred was talking with him, the young man started shaking. Suddenly, his body levitated out of the hammock, flipped over, and fell to the ground dead. This might seem hard for some to

Journey into the Unknown

believe, but that is the power of witchcraft. The Piaroa tribe was bound by this. When one person had a serious problem against another one, he went to the witchdoctor who put a spell on the other person causing problems. The cursed person became sick and knew that someone had put a spell on him. That person then went to another witchdoctor and asked him to counteract the spell put on him. Thus, began the battle of the witchdoctors, ending when one dies.

As the Piaroas came to know the true God, they had lots of questions for us. Through these conversations, we discovered the basics of their old beliefs. For the presentation of the Gospel, this was a good starting point. When explaining the Gospel, we never took something away from a culture or belief without replacing it with something better. We had to show them the difference between the gods they feared and our God that they didn't need to fear. To do this, we compared their creation story to God's Biblical account.

Their creation story had similarities and differences from God's that we were able to use. According to the witchdoctors, the beginning of the Piaroa Tribe started on the Cuao River in the Amazonas State of southern Venezuela.

> *There first appeared a man called Mųio'cą who was alone. From his right eye he made a brother, Huäjäri, and from his left eye he made a sister. Chejeru and Mųio'cą was left blind and turned into a deer. Time progressed and Huäjäri took the Bocon fish and made a head from a gourd and arms and legs of mud. He then blew in them breath, and this was the beginning of the*

Death Brings Life

Piaroa people. Time progressed and the sister, Chejeru, moved away with a white man (anyone who was not Piaroa).

Due to population growth, the air became very heavy and hard to breath. The Piaroas tried to raise the sky using every method known to them but were unable to do so. They then asked for Chejeru's people to help them, and they agreed to try. Huäjäri decided to go visit his sister, Chejeru. At the end of his visit, finding his brother-in-law away from home, he violated his sister and left. Upon her husband's return, she told him what her brother had done to her. He then chased Huäjäri, killed him, and returned home. However, Huäjäri came back to life and returned to his home.

Tapir

Years later, Huäjäri decided to visit his sister again and upon leaving repeated the same behavior as before, violating his sister yet again. Once again when her husband found out about it, he chased Huäjäri down to kill him, but this time he took drastic measures to ensure his death. He cut him up into pieces and then boiled him in a cooking pot. He returned home to his wife, Chejeru. Huäjäri came back to life again, but as a Tapir. This animal became their creator and god. They worshiped him to the point of never eating this type of animal. If a Tapir

Journey into the Unknown

> *walked through their garden plot, they set aside any plant that it touched. They would not eat of those plants.*

When we worked through their creation story, there were many similarities we used to explain the Gospel. However, when we came to the place where Huäjäri violated his own sister, a repugnant sin to everyone in the tribe, we had a huge difference between Huäjäri and God. Huäjäri committed a terrible sin, but our God was and is sinless. As we drew comparisons and contrasts, we had an opening for the Gospel.

The Piaroas had lived their whole lives in fear of the evil spirits and without any hope. When we took God's Word to them and told them about the only true living God and about His Son, Jesus, who came to this earth and died for their sins, they had hope and through their belief, they had eternal life in Heaven.

As we shared the Gospel, the ministry grew exponentially, and we quickly realized the need to prepare church leaders in the villages to evangelize their own people and plant churches. These church leaders were needed to take the Gospel to the seventy percent of the Piaroa tribe located in the restricted areas. We constantly looked for new believers that demonstrated a fierce desire to know God's Word and to reach others with the Gospel. We also looked for those who manifested the qualifications set down in I Timothy 3:1-7. We dedicated time to these men to ground them in the Word.

Eventually, many churches were planted throughout the tribe. Fred taught them about leadership and discipling

Death Brings Life

others. He made trips out to villages and taught Bible seminars to representatives from the local tribal churches. For the Piaroa church leaders, some of these trips took up to five days of travel, as they had to walk through the jungle to the location. The Piaroas would spend up to ten hours a day asking questions and listening to the teachers. One time, Fred was so tired that he went to his hammock and fell right to sleep once he finished speaking. The Piaroas talked amongst themselves about what they were learning until they couldn't stand it any longer. They then woke up Fred to ask him more questions. What a hunger for the Word of God!

When we see the Lord working with many positive results, Satan does not stand by without throwing his fiery darts. In one such seminar, this became very evident. Fred

Seminar Teaching

taught a seminar at the headwaters of the Cuao River. There were about 20 leaders present. They were there four days with intensive ten-hour-a-day teaching. In these seminars, they talked about many different subjects as the teaching sessions allowed for them to ask any question they might have about any subject.

At one of the seminars, they were discussing dreams and visions. Some leaders shared stories they had heard or experienced. One story was about a twelve-year-old girl who said she "went to heaven" and came back. According

Journey into the Unknown

to her, they would have everything in heaven that they have here, outboard motors, motorcycles, cars and on and on. Another story was about a middle-aged woman who said she "went to heaven" and came back. She said she received a message from Jesus. He told her that he was coming back on a specific day. She gave the date and the location she believed Jesus would come back and said that whoever was not in that village on that date would not go to heaven. Oh, the havoc this caused as people began leaving their villages to travel to where Jesus was coming. Pots, pans, dogs, and everything else they owned they took with them. As they traveled, they realized their heavy loads would not be needed when Jesus came, so they threw away their belongings along the trails to the village. On the specific date, Jesus did not come back, and a large group of believers and nonbelievers had lost everything.

Shortly after these "visions," one of the main topics of questions and teaching was on who God is and who Satan is and how each works in our lives; God to help us and Satan to deceive us. They were deep in discussion when they heard the makeshift door to the house make a clicking sound. When they heard the clicking sound, they thought that it was kids playing around the door outside and one of the men went to tell them to play elsewhere so they would not interrupt the teaching. To Fred and the other leaders' amazement, the man could not open the door. Thinking that the kids had propped it shut with a pole from the outside, he called to the people outside to move it but there was nothing against the door. Neither the people inside nor those outside could get the door opened. They realized what was happening and prayed to rebuke Satan and his

Death Brings Life

power. While praying, the door made a clicking sound again and opened a bit so that it would move freely.

This led to long conversations about the power of Satan versus the power of God and was a great lesson to this group of church leaders who not very long ago lived lives bound by witchcraft and evil spirit worship. Their faith in God was strengthened seeing how even the power of Satan yielded to the power of God.

> *".... greater is He that is in you than He that is in the World." I John 4:4*

As the missionaries taught people, many came to the knowledge of Jesus Christ and accepted Him as their Savior. The church grew and other churches

Commissioning Missionaries

were planted throughout the tribe. Church leaders were taught and installed in new churches. The new churches eventually sent out their own missionaries to areas where no one had ever gone. Plane crashes, death, witchcraft, weariness, government restrictions, Satan; none of these were a match for God's plan for the Piaroas!

Journey into the Unknown

Chapter 11 – Changes and Time Out

We continued to make plans for reaching out to more of the villages that we had been in contact with during the crash search. Piaroas from these areas were making their way over mountains, across rivers and through jungles to beg for someone to come and teach them. These trips lasted from five to eight days depending on the season. Since we were alone, with all the government projects and the problems of the people and an epidemic of measles on an adjoining river, the need for more help was great.

Fred made a five-day trip to various areas where the measles epidemic broke out, and he treated almost 60 people and sent medicine to other places where we could not go. In all, there were about ten deaths from measles complications. When he arrived back in San Juan, he found us involved in an epidemic of whooping cough.

Finally, another family, Ron and Avis Bodin, joined the Piaroa team. The possibility of having personnel live in remote areas became a reality. We now had three families and four single ladies involved in language study, teaching, and translation.

We were without a Piaroa team leader since Curt's death. Our mission chairman, Bob Shaylor, asked Fred if he would take his dad's leadership role of the Piaroa team. Fred immediately agreed. As team leader, he would be responsible to make contacts in the villages. He also would arrange for missionaries to go and live in the villages. Lastly, he would make periodic visits to each missionary and encourage them in their work. So, as a family, we made

Changes and Time Out

plans to temporarily return to the village of Punta Piaroa where the work first started. We planned to spend time teaching, translating and encouraging while Fred led the team.

During the time after Curt's death, our family back in the States was asking that we come home for a short time. Both of Fred's grandparents were declining in health, and his grandpa never got over Curt's death. He was in the hospital with fluid around his heart and was not expected to live. They wanted to see our daughter, Melanie, who was Grandma Findley's first great granddaughter. We felt that we, along with Allie Lee, should return to the States for a few months. When we arrived home, Fred's grandpa was in a coma, but woke up long enough to recognize us and meet his great granddaughter, Melanie, for the first time. Four days later Grandpa Findley was reunited with his son in Heaven. After eight months, we returned to Venezuela.

A few months after returning to the field, our field administrator, Don Bodin, called by radio and asked to talk with Fred. I thought it was strange when he didn't give me the message, stating he preferred to set a time when Fred could talk with him instead. We soon discovered the reason; he needed to give me bad news about my dad. Don wanted to make sure Fred was with me when I received the news.

My dad had worked for years as a supervising technician in the Laboratories Department of the International Nickel Company and was in his last year before retirement. He was asked to fill in on another job while most of the workers were on a vacation due to a factory shut-down. His temporary job was to climb up to the top of a large tank and

Journey into the Unknown

inspect the gauges to make sure they were functioning properly. Unfortunately, they had not, and a pipe swung around and hit him in the head knocking him off of an eleven-foot tank. He landed on his head leaving him paralyzed from the neck down.

I wanted so much to talk with my mom to know more about it and to find out if she wanted me to come home to help her take care of him. To talk with her, we had to make a four-day trip downriver to Puerto Ayacucho where we could talk by phone to the U.S. Those were hard days, but once again God proved to us that His grace was sufficient. When I could communicate with my mom, she assured me that there was nothing I could do at that time. She had moved into the hospital room with him and would be staying with him until he was released. Three months later he was released, and she took care of him at home for the next 21 years as he was left a quadriplegic. She claimed the verse, *"This sickness is not unto death but for the glory of God, that the Son of God may be glorified through it." John 11:4.* My parents never once asked me to leave the mission field and come home to help take care of my dad. The Lord also gave me peace about staying.

Many have since testified that my parents' lives were a blessing to them from a young age until he took them home to glory. It would take another book to tell how they dedicated their lives to the Lord and how He used them in so many ways, before and after the accident, during the hard times as well as the good times. How blessed we both were to have parents that gave their all to serve the Lord. What great examples they were to us, and still are!

Changes and Time Out

Since we decided to not go home to the States, we continued with our original plans and moved to Punta Piaroa. We attended our annual field conference in TamaTama. A field conference is a time when all our personnel came together to fellowship and make plans and decisions for the upcoming year in the different ministries. Fred was also installed as a member of the field leadership team which was responsible for all the New Tribes missionaries in Venezuela. This filled the last vacancy left open by his father's death. This once again added more responsibility on Fred as he met with the other leaders sharing the weight of overseeing the different works. As they talked over the future of the Piaroa team and its growth, the question of home assignments came up. They needed to figure out how to stagger them so that just one family at a time was out of the country. Since I was again pregnant, and with the recent news of my dad's accident, the field leadership team suggested that we should go back to the States a couple months earlier than our originally planned furlough. I was six months pregnant already and could not fly after the eighth month.

We returned to the States the end of January 1969, and our baby boy, Brian Lee, arrived the last day of March. We were so happy to have a boy as we now had one of each. His Grandpa Wilson, my dad, was so proud of him. He

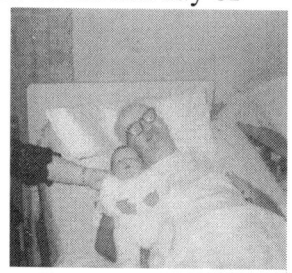

Brian as a Newborn

Brian with Grandpa

Journey into the Unknown

could not hold him and the only way he could feel him was by putting him on the pillow next to his face...the only place in his body that had feeling. The look on Dad's face will always stay with me. It was hard seeing Dad so disabled, but at the same time such a joy to see how he had accepted it. It was a great testimony to so many who came to encourage him. The rest of our home assignment was spent with them and a lot of traveling with a toddler and a new baby while we visited supporting churches and family.

Journey into the Unknown

Chapter 12 – New Open Doors

The Chivapure

While we were in the States, the unreached areas of the Piaroa tribe continued to open. We received many pleas from them to send missionaries to teach and tell people in these other Piaroa villages more about God. One Sunday morning service, a young man walked in wearing just a loin cloth and sat through the service with eager ears to hear the Word. After the service, he approached Allie Lee Findley and Kathy Earle. The first thing he said was, "When is someone coming to teach us?" They did not know the man and started asking him questions. They found out that he had walked four days to ask if someone would come to their village. He told them that many from his village wanted to hear about God. He was the third one to come out from that area to ask for help. It was a very difficult place for two middle aged women to travel to. However, they felt the burden to do what they could to get to some of these villages.

The two ladies went to the Chivapure River area for a time. Allie Lee later wrote:

> *Our trip to the headwaters of the Chivapure River was a blessing and privilege as well as a nightmare in getting there. Many of the people in San Juan felt the trail was too bad and steep for us to climb and discouraged us from going saying we would never make it and would have to turn back. However,*

New Open Doors

we felt the Lord had opened the way and we should at least try. We got together a few things we felt we would need to take and asked six men from San Juan to go with us to take it over the trail. The first day and a half we went by canoe, the men cutting through at least five big trees that had fallen across the river. The first night we slept in the jungle and by noon the second day the trees and vines were hanging so thickly over the river, they made it impossible to go any further by canoe. So, we started out by trail.

Allie Lee and Kathy

The next two days we walked across hot grassland areas, waded through the big river twice, waded through 12 creeks, and walked up a mountain all day just stopping to rest when we felt that we couldn't drag one foot in front of the other. Our food

Dugout Canoe

Journey into the Unknown

for those three days was "glop". Glop was a mixture of raw oatmeal, powdered milk and "toddy" (a chocolate malt powder) mixed with water.

The next day we arrived at the village. The people were very happy to see us but somewhat surprised that we had made it over the trail. The captain had them build us a house with just a roof (no walls) and we were soon settled in. We hung our hammocks, made a couple of pole tables to put our things on, arranged a couple of rocks from the river bank for seats. and stacked a nice pile of firewood that the women had brought so we could cook over an open fire.

We had a service the first night with three of the men that went with us. We shared the Word of God, and they listened with much interest. The next day our carriers left for San Juan, and Kathy and I were left with our new friends and away from all outside contact. Classes were soon started which met every morning and afternoon and we conducted a service every night...

At the end of the trip, nineteen had accepted the Lord as their Savior. The trials weren't easy in the coming months as the new believers faced sickness and death. They were so new in the Lord with no one to encourage them in their faith or help them

New Open Doors

resist the witchdoctors and evil spirits. Their instincts were to trust the witchdoctor, but now that they were believers in Christ their lives were turned upside down. Who would help these new babes in Christ? We had no answer to that, but we prayed the Lord would put it on the heart of those He wanted to go.

The arduous trip these two ladies took to this new area, resulted in God answering prayer and sometime later Larry and Valerie Bockus and family moved into the Chivapure River area and after a time saw a new church of believers established there. Sometimes we were faced with hard things to do but God was always faithful and was there with us each step of the way.

The Yuanas

For years, there were rumors of so-called "other people" besides the Piaroas living in the jungles in the surrounding areas of San Juan. Some Piaroas had been out hunting and had found abandoned houses and old trails. They had told Curt about it, and he, Fred, and some other men from the village spent several days in the jungle looking for the "other people" but found no one. The years passed without any contact with these mysterious people.

Ten years later, a group of Piaroas went downriver to hunt for a few days. While they were downriver, they ran into a group of 12 "other people" in the jungle. They convinced three of the twelve to get in the boat to go see the missionaries. Allie Lee had finished teaching a class when she heard their boat. Someone ran up to the door and called

Journey into the Unknown

for her. Allie Lee came out and saw the villagers. It turned out they weren't Piaroas as she had expected; these were some of the "other people" that Fred and his Dad had tried to find. They were rumored to be people that killed outsiders. However, rather than being ruthless, they seemed friendly. Over the next few days, word spread and people from the nearby villages came by canoe to see the "other people." They were lighter skinned than the Piaroas and had no clothes, just loin cloth. The men and women alike had long black hair. They spoke an unfamiliar language. No one could understand them even though there were five different tribal language groups living among the Piaroas. From sign language, we understood their closest village was six or seven days walk, and there were many people in their village.

Yuana Tribesman

During this initial contact with the Yuanas, two of our missionary men, one a linguist, along with five of the Piaroas tried to put the Yuanas' words into writing as best they could to compare with the written languages of other tribes. It became clear that years of work would be needed to put this language into writing as it was completely different. They began praying for a family with linguistic abilities to live with the Yuanas. We needed someone that could learn a language and put it into writing. This process would take a long time. Tom and Lila Blinco were chosen to go to the Yuanas since Lila was proficient in languages and had worked in this role in another tribe.

New Open Doors

Since the Blincos did not speak or understand the Yuana language, they would have no way of communicating with the people. They would have to learn the language by immersing themselves in the villagers' daily lives. They would be isolated from the outside world, from other missionaries, from any resources, except for a short-wave radio operated by batteries with which they could receive messages from the mission headquarters at a set hour in the morning.

It took two days by river for the Blinco family, Fred, and the Piaroa helpers to get to the place where they could go no further by boat. From there they walked two more days through the jungle. They crossed smaller rivers and creeks with no bridges...sometimes with the water up to their shoulders. Everything they took with them had to be carried in backpacks and one of the Piaroa women carried the Blinco's daughter all the way. When the 17 of them walked out of the jungle into the Yuana village clearing for the first time, they didn't know what to expect. Because there were 17 outsiders coming into their village, this visit could be misconstrued as threatening and trouble could ensue. Surprisingly, the Yuana fled to the jungle once they saw the missionary team except for one man who had a broken toe and could not run. He sat on a large rock and shook with fear. No one knew what was going to happen next. Did they really kill outsiders? Would they kill the missionary party out of fear before they even saw their faces? Fred, the Blincos, and the Piaroas stood completely still in the middle of the village clearing and waited.

Finally, the Yuana men sent some of their children back in to the village from their hiding places. They waited to see

Journey into the Unknown

how the children would be received. Eventually, the women were sent in. They were followed by the men once the men realized it was safe. Still no one knew exactly what was going to happen. So, the mission party tried communicating with them through sign language. They did their best to explain they wanted to stay in their village and make a house for the Blincos. They had entered the village mid-morning and by mid-afternoon, the men were helping make a small palm house for the Blinco family to stay in. Fred and the Piaroas stayed with them three days and then left Tom, Lila, and their young daughter by themselves. They took the only boat and returned to San Juan. Every month or so someone went back to the village and checked on Tom and Lila.

Tom worked with some of the men in the village and cut down trees to make a clearing for an airdrop. A small one engine mission plane could fly over, dip down, and drop food to them in this area. These airdrops were exciting trips. The pilot took the passenger door off the plane. At the site, the pilot slowed the plane as much as possible and then flew over the tree tops. At just the right moment, he told the person with him to push out a couple of boxes as he pulled the plane up and over the trees. This was repeated until they had dropped all the food to those below. It was quite a thrill for those who pushed the boxes out the door! The force of the wind through the open door sometimes shredded the shirt of the person pushing the boxes out of the plane.

To protect the products being delivered by airdrops, the food had to be tied in several boxes and then put in cloth bags, so it wouldn't burst open when it hit the ground. No matter how many precautions were taken, there were still

New Open Doors

occasions when things didn't go as planned. One time, there was a large box of sugar in the plane. It was dropped correctly, but it burst upon impact. Once the villagers found out it was sugar, they started squatting on the ground eating the sugar off the ground. They were having a feast on the airstrip! Another time, a box containing both dry beans and gun shot was dropped. When it hit the ground, the beans and gunshot combined. The missionaries who were waiting for them spent a great deal of time and patience picking the gunshot out of the dried beans!

Once the airdrops started, land visits were reduced to every three months. Once the airstrip was cleared, the airdrops were not needed in that area. So, Tom, with the help of the Yuanas, cleaned out and constructed a small runway so the plane could land near him. Tom and Lila now had constant contact with the rest of the mission. Sometime after the airstrip was finished, the Wes Kennedy family joined the Blinco family as part of the Yuana team. Tom and Lila had completed the initial language breakdown and language learning alone, but now had coworkers.

This was the beginning of working with the "other people."

The Maco Tribe

Shortly after returning from home assignment in the early 70s, we were on our way to TamaTama on the Ventuari River, one of the main rivers we traveled between the Manapiare River and the Orinoco River. We hit a rock hidden under the surface of the water. As a result, the foot of our outboard motor was broken. We were out in the middle of nowhere in a speed boat without a paddle! We started floating downriver and used the lid of a Styrofoam

Journey into the Unknown

cooler to keep us in the middle of the river. Darkness was nearing. After eight hours of floating with our three-year-old on board, we sighted some tribal people. They were at the edge of the river in a canoe with an outboard motor on it. Despite their limited understanding of Spanish and the Piaroa language, we arranged with them to tow us to the nearest settlement. This was our first contact with the Maco tribe. The Piaroas often talked about them and referred to these villagers as distant relatives.

Maco Tribespeople

We often thought about the Maco people and the need for a team of missionaries to work with them. Then one year at a Piaroa Bible conference, we heard a report that the Piaroas had taken it upon themselves to take the Gospel to the Maco. When a Piaroa woman married one of the Maco men, some of the Piaroas learned to speak the Maco language and in return some of the Maco people learned to speak the Piaroa language. The Piaroas were able to share the Gospel with them in a very simple way, and some of the Maco accepted the Lord. We were eventually invited to teach a church leaders' seminar in the Maco village for those who had become bilingual.

We counted it a real privilege when we were asked to conduct a survey of this tribe. We needed to find out as much as possible concerning their spiritual needs in order to place a team of missionaries with them. Fred, along with a Venezuelan missionary and a Christian doctor, flew into

New Open Doors

San Juan. From there they traveled the same river we had floated down to the Maco village of Caño Marueta. They also branched out and visited six other Maco villages. The Maco were considered semi-civilized due to their contact with civilization. Except for what the Piaroas had shared with them in the last few years, they had been without the Gospel. We were overjoyed to hear them express their desire for missionaries to learn their language and teach them more about God's Word. However, the amount of Bible truth they could grasp through the Piaroa language was limited, and many of them didn't understand at all.

Several years later a team was formed and moved into the Maco tribe. Both the Yuana and Maco tribes had great teams working together to learn the language, plant churches, and do Bible translation.

Journey into the Unknown

Chapter 13 – First Contact

In 1964 two young Piaroa boys arrived in San Juan and with wide grins explained that they had come from the Parguaza River and wanted to learn to read God's Word. They had heard that in San Juan the Piaroas knew about God. We gave them literacy books and taught them how to use them. Gonzalo, one of the boys, had a desire to learn and within a few weeks had finished the first reading book. One day, however, he didn't show up for class. We inquired about him and were told that he had left and was on his way back to the Parguaza River. This would have been a 15-day walk for him. Time went by and Gonzalo was forgotten. However, in 1969, Fred received a letter from him with a plea to "come and teach us about God." We discussed and prayed about this request as a team. We were stretched to the limit with our Piaroa work. We could not see how we could spare the few missionaries that we had to start a new work in the Parguaza. After praying for weeks with the plea from Gonzalo, God gave us peace. We decided we would trust the Lord and made plans to move to the Parguaza.

The first step in making this move was to have an aerial survey conducted to locate the many villages and their proximity to a river. The Lord provided a pilot, Dennis Blue, who worked in one of the larger cities in Venezuela. Dennis was a born-again believer and wanted to use his time and his one-engine, six passenger plane to serve the Lord. He offered to take Fred on a survey trip when it was needed.

First Contact

As we, the Piaroa team, were making plans for the surveys and the move, Fred wrote:

> *As we were making plans, we were talking with some of the Piaroas in TamaTama. A young fellow, Santiago, was there and seemed very anxious to go with me, as several years back we had talked about a possible trip down there and he expressed his desire to go. We did not give too much thought to the possibility of his going with me as the trip would initiate in San Juan and he was in TamaTama, some four days by river travel from San Juan. In July, we received word that Santiago had come over to Caño Marietta, less than a day travel from San Juan and close to where we would be passing by. As we look back over the trip and see how the Lord worked things out for Santiago to go, we can only praise the Lord for His leading and guidance.*

Village In Jungle

During the aerial survey, they found many villages, some relatively close to the river and some that would involve several days of walking. After the aerial survey was completed, the team felt that a land survey would be beneficial to determine in which village to start teaching the people. To make this land survey possible, they had to take our small boat from San Juan to Puerto Ayacucho. From there it was transported by truck for 45 miles to circumvent a long stretch of dangerous, unnavigable rapids. After that, it

Journey into the Unknown

would be two days by boat to get to the Parguaza River people. They would be close to where the Piaroas and Gonzalo's family lived.

On the way, they stopped to visit Señor Micoliche who had lived in a settlement called "El Carmen" on the Parguaza River for thirty years. This gentleman had a working relationship with the Piaroas from this area and knew a lot about the history from there. His counsel was, "I am glad you are coming, but you will never accomplish anything with these people. You and your family will suffer much, because these people can't be trusted. They lie, steal, kill and you just can't teach them anything." Then he told the long story about the young man that had hung his grandmother.

> *Granny was in a hut in my yard, very sick and at the point of death. We had been doctoring her and felt that she was on her way to recovery. One day we heard her small granddaughter screaming that they had killed her grandmother. When we ran into the hut, old granny was hanging from the overhead crossbeams. Her grandson had sneaked in and without warning had tied a rope around her neck and hung her. To his way of thinking, she was too sick to travel, and too old to live longer.*

The grandson in this story was the same young man, Gonzalo, who had gone to San Juan to learn to read and had returned home without his telling us. He also later sent a letter asking for someone to come tell his people about God.

First Contact

After leaving Sr. Micoliche's place, they arrived at the first Piaroa village at 5:30 p.m. Leaving their hammocks in the boat, they went into the village to see what kind of reception they would receive. The people seemed surprised to see them but were friendly enough. When asked where they were going to sleep, Fred and Santiago told them they would like to sleep with them in their communal hut. They agreed to this. One of the young men went back to the boat with them to get their things and showed them a place to hang their hammocks in the back corner of the hut. They thought this was strange, as generally visitors are always put in the center of the house at night, but they hung their hammocks where they were told.

As the evening progressed, things seemed to be going as expected. Santiago and Fred were talking to the people and Santiago found out that he had some relatives in the village...two older women. He began talking with them about their family and telling them news of his family while Fred continued talking to the men. As they were talking, the men started sniffing dope and getting high. This was part of their witchcraft rituals to ward off evil spirits. In the meantime, Santiago was talking with his relatives, and they wanted to know why he had brought a person that eats Piaroas into their village. He asked them what they were talking about. They said they were told by the witchdoctor that the white people would fly over their villages in airplanes to find them and then would come back by river later to kill and eat the children.

Santiago assured them this was not true. He told them they would not harm them, and he and Fred wanted to come and live with them to teach them about God. After a while, the

Journey into the Unknown

women told Santiago that the men were going to kill him and Fred that night after they went to sleep. When Santiago heard this, he went over to Fred and told him. Santiago also had found out that the men had two shotguns hidden in the outside palm walls of the hut. Fred feared for his life and vowed to fight as he was not ready to give up his wife and family yet.

Fred and Santiago began talking in Spanish about the situation, so the villagers would not understand what they were saying. As they talked, the men continued to take their dope and chant all night. The only thing that remained then for Fred and Santiago to do was to commit the entire thing into the Lord's hands and try to get some sleep. However, sleep was hard to come by that night for Fred. Oddly enough, Santiago lay down in his hammock and went straight to sleep. Fred became irritated as he remained awake. So, he finally woke Santiago and asked how he could sleep knowing that they were going to be killed that night. Santiago's answer was simple. He said: "if they kill me tonight, tomorrow I will wake up in heaven with Jesus." After that, Fred prayed, committed the situation to the Lord, and went to sleep as well.

Pulling Boat Through Rapids

When dawn came, they both awoke and went outside the house to talk about things privately. As they were talking, two young men came outside and each pulled a shotgun

First Contact

from the palm leaf walls. They turned around and took the guns back inside the hut! The Lord in His goodness spared Fred and Santiago, and they received a little warmer reception that morning. One of the young men that was to do the shooting the night before was their guide upriver that day. He also turned out to be a relative of Santiago's.

As they traveled upriver, high water and bad rapids prevented them from getting to one of the main villages they had planned to visit. However, they felt the Lord had His hand in this also, because the captain of this village was known to be the most feared witchdoctor in that area. The villagers also had a couple shotguns in waiting for any white man that visited. Fred and Santiago soon found out that all the villages along the river had guns for this reason.

The next day, they visited Caño Pendare and received a very warm welcome because Santiago had relatives there as well. This village, in contrast to the one they had stayed in the night before, wanted them to come back and live with them. Due to a welcoming attitude, Fred and Santiago decided that we as a family should move to this village. Here we could work and reach out into the other villages. We desired to give them the Word of God which could deliver them from the fear and grip that Satan had on them. Before leaving, arrangements were made with Captain Prinio, of Pendare, and the other leaders in the village for our return. They granted us permission to build a palm house for our family.

We praised the Lord for the way that He gave Santiago the desire to go and the way that He worked things out for him to be there. He had relatives in every village we visited. We felt that the Lord used Santiago's presence to stay the hands

Journey into the Unknown

of those that wanted to kill them, realizing of course that only those things that the Lord allows can happen.

Fred and Santiago returned to San Juan. The children and I were anxious to see him. We had no idea at that time how close he came to not returning to us. It was only the grace of God that kept him safe. So, we happily celebrated Melanie's 5th birthday, and shortly after, we celebrated the wedding of Santiago and Maria. They had both a traditional Piaroa wedding and a Christian wedding ceremony.

Christian Piaroa Wedding

Traditional Piaroa Wedding

Chapter 14 – Move into Parguaza River Area

A couple months later Fred returned to Caño Pendare to build a temporary palm house with the help of the men there. The house was divided into two large rooms. The front part was the kitchen and sitting room area and the back half was the sleeping area which later became two rooms. At my request, we put one small window frame in to give more light. Fred then returned to Puerto Ayacucho to pick-up the kids and me, Allie Lee, her co-worker Kathy Earle, Santiago, and Maria, Santiago's wife.

We left Puerto Ayacucho at 9 A.M. on January 5, 1971 by truck to El Carmen. This was the settlement where Sr. Micoliche lived and was as far as we could travel by road. We were loaded down in a 3/4-ton pick-up. Fred and I, with the children, sat in the back of the truck under a tarp with the cargo. Kathy and Allie Lee sat in front. The sand from the road nearly suffocated us, and we had to stop several times on the way to breathe good air. We finally took part of the tarp off the roof to get more wind and less dust. We expected our truck ride to the Parguaza to take only four hours.

Along with us were two national men that the driver wanted to take to help him on the way back. Also accompanying us was Steve Dawson, an MK, who offered to help. There were four bridges in all to cross. The last one was so broken and damaged that it couldn't be used, thus we had to find a shallow spot we could drive through. We were thankful that it wasn't raining while we waited the 3 1/2 hours for the men to get the truck unstuck as they tried

Move into Parguaza River Area

to cross the caño. We were also thankful for a nice bathing place where the children could spend some time playing in the water while we waited. This helped the time pass, but they did get badly bitten by gnats. Fred forgot about his billfold in his pocket until it was all wet, so he spread it out on the ground to dry while continuing to work getting the truck out. When they finally got the truck out, we quickly went on our way. We were almost at El Carmen when Fred remembered the billfold and had to return to the caño to get it. Finally, we arrived at El Carmen and two Piaroa men were waiting for us. They took one canoe load of our things up that night to our house in Caño Pendare, and then returned in the morning for us and the rest of our supplies. We spent the first night at Sr. Micolichi's place. The next morning, we traveled by dug-out canoe to Caño Pendare for three hours. We then had a five-minute walk through the jungles from the Parguaza River to where the house was located. We were right next to the main village house. We could hear the Piaroas talk all the time and they could hear us!

Move to Parguaza River

The next day Allie Lee and Kathy along with Santiago and Maria continued up the Parguaza River to the village of Maraca, where the people had previously said that they could live with them. They met the people from this village coming down river to hunt for

Journey into the Unknown

the tree bark that they used to make their dope. They stopped and talked to the two ladies and Santiago and Maria. The captain told them that they did not want to learn God's Word and did not want them in their village. Since Fred knew from the aerial survey trip that there was a large village above the rapids, they started for that village. After pulling the canoe through three rapids, they arrived at Bonifacio's village in the late afternoon of the second day. They knew that he, the chief, was the most feared witchdoctor in that area and the most rebellious, so it was with a shaky feeling that they entered the village clearing.

They heard a man standing outside the house call to those on the inside that "the one's we don't want have arrived". This did not help their shaky feelings. When they entered the house all the people were standing there staring at "two strange white women." After the initial shock of wondering what was about to happen, the people began talking with them and it turned into a nice visit. The chief was friendly and gave them some bananas to eat but let them know that he was not interested in God's Word and did not want them in their village. To emphasize this, he would not let them sleep in their village and they had to sleep in the jungle on the other side of the river.

Back in the village of Pendare, where we were, we continued to unpack and arrange things in the house so that we could start teaching literacy. In our palm house, our kitchen table and benches were made of split palms, and we had a piece of plywood on the table for an even table top. It worked. Fred made shelves and cupboards to store our food and dishes in to keep our supplies out of sight and out of mind. He also made split palm shelves around the wall in

Move into Parguaza River Area

the kitchen for the camp stove, dishes and work area. He and the villagers built split palm benches around the walls in the sitting area. The villagers just came right in and sat down on the split tree benches and watched us. They watched our every move, talked about it, and laughed a lot. Everything was so strange about us, and they never tired of watching while we did our work. We knew how it felt to be in a cage at the zoo!

Fred Teaching Literacy

During the day, the sitting area served as a school room where we taught them to read and write in their own language using a home-made chalk board. Every evening, we used the sitting area as a place for our church meetings. The whole village would turn out for these meetings as they were so ready to hear about the God that we had come to tell them about.

We never had a minute to ourselves until they left for the night. One day while we were trying to have a "siesta" in the afternoon, we heard some voices out in the sitting area. This surprised us as we had the make-shift door hooked from the inside.

Piaroas Studying

Journey into the Unknown

It turned out the kids had come through the open, screenless, window. So, for more privacy, we later put a screen on the window. That did not stop them from getting in, however. After we put in a screen, the adults found a way around the screen. They sent a small kid through the dry palm leaf walls to open the door and let the rest of them in. It was never-ending, and we just had to accept it.

At Pendare, we didn't have any gnats and only a few mosquitoes at night which was a real blessing. It kept the children from having so many infections, and they didn't have to wear long sleeves during the heat of the day while playing outside. There were little flies that were pesky and swarmed around our eyes. That was still a lot better than the blood sucking gnats. We also had a nice caño close to the house where we bathed and washed clothes. The swimming hole was quite shallow and had a sandy bottom; it made a lovely place for the children to swim and play. Melanie would have lived in it if I would have let her. However, the water was quite cold at night, and we had to cut down on her time in the caño. I enjoyed going down and washing clothes while the children played in the water. Sometimes we went as a family and everyone helped wash clothes. Even two-year old Brian would try to rub the clothes together like he really knew how to wash them. The clothes washing took a lot of time. When we started classes, I had to get teenage girls to do it for me. They were glad for the opportunity to earn some spending money. Upriver from the swimming hole was fresh, clean water as no one lived above it. This was our running water. We paid some boys to go with the buckets to the stream and "run" water back for us.

Move into Parguaza River Area

Our third night there, as we listened to our transistor radio, we heard that a missionary doctor and his wife had arrived in Puerto Ayacucho for a short time. They wanted to visit a ministry that was just beginning and was a "frontier" area. They were hoping to set up clinics in these villages to care for the sick. Different areas asked if they could come to their village, but due to the distance and expenses involved in flying them there and back, they didn't see how they could do it. It was then suggested that maybe they try to go to the Parguaza River. We quickly realized we might get visitors soon in our new house! So, we set several alarm clocks that evening to make sure we didn't miss the next morning broadcast. We wished many times that we had a two-way radio to communicate with the outside, but there was none available for us.

As we listened to the transistor radio the next morning, TamaTama, Parima and other stations asked if the doctor could come to their villages. Ed Killam, who was our acting field administrator, finally answered the people calling in and said, "No, the doctor and his wife will be going to the Parguaza River." We jumped out of our hammocks, heads spinning. We had just sent our boat and smaller motor upriver with Kathy and Allie Lee leaving us with no way to pick up the doctor and his wife. While we were trying to figure out what to do, we heard Ed say, "Attention Fred, you will be having some company today. You are to meet them at Sr. Micolichis place (in El Carmen) at 10:30 a.m.," and then he repeated the message a couple more times. He also said that a plane would circle over our house and drop a note to meet the doctors in case we missed the radio message. It was an hour and a half to El Carmen with a canoe using a 40 h.p. motor, but we only

Journey into the Unknown

had the Piaroas' paddling canoes (which could not hold a motor). So, Fred and Steve, along with several men, started paddling down river. They took with them a 40 h.p. motor just in case they could borrow a canoe made for an outboard motor. Meanwhile I wrote in big letters on the chalk board "JIM WAIT FRED COMING". When Jim, the pilot, circled over the house, he tipped the airplane's wing to acknowledge he saw my note. This was exciting to everyone except for Brian who being only two years old was scared by the sound of the airplane as it buzzed us.

It took Fred and the others four hours to paddle down river to the airstrip. They were able to borrow a boat from Sr. Micolichi in El Carmen to bring the doctor, Bill, and his wife back. As the plane was delayed several hours, Fred arrived at the airstrip about the same time that the plane landed. The Canadian doctor, Bill, and his wife, Sharon, were a young couple still in their twenties and very much interested in the mission field. They had been in the West Indies for three months and were on their way to Africa to work in a hospital affiliated with the

Doctor Explaining Instructions

Move into Parguaza River Area

African Indian Mission. We certainly hadn't expected to have company where we were located, much less so soon after arriving ourselves, but we really enjoyed having them visit and wouldn't have wanted to miss the privilege. They were very adaptable to the circumstances in the jungle and were just plain "good sports."

Allie Lee and Kathy returned unexpectedly that same night. We thought they had heard the message on the radio and had come down to greet our guests, but they were shocked when they arrived and found us with visitors. They had returned to pick up more of the supplies they had stored in our palm hut. Once they arrived, Kathy and Allie Lee decided that while they were in Pendare, they would go to visit another village just a four hour walk away. So, they also spent the night. Our little house was overflowing with nine people that night. The next day we spent visiting together and making plans for taking the doctor around to different villages. We also hoped that bringing a doctor into the villages would create goodwill. We soon found that the Piaroas on the Parguaza River were very different from the ones we had worked with in San Juan and TamaTama. They seemed like a completely different tribe of people, except for the language. Much of the time they were taking dope and doing witchcraft.

The following morning Fred, Steve, the doctor, his wife, I, and several Piaroas left for upriver. Allie Lee and Kathy stayed back in Pendare with the kids. We were so thankful that they had arrived unexpectedly. We visited several villages on our way up but planned on spending more time coming downriver so the doctor could treat the sick. As we went upriver, we had three sets of rapids to go through. At

Journey into the Unknown

the first two, the boat had to be unloaded and everything carried around on land while the men pulled the boat through the rapids. After they got the boat through and all was safe, they had a good time playing in the water and swimming in the rapids before reloading the boat.

When we could go no further by boat, we waded through the caño carrying all our supplies. Eventually, we went by trail up a small mountain and down the other side. We then crossed another caño and a hill. At 3:30 p.m, we finally reached the village of Captain Bonafacio, the feared witch doctor.

The tribal people stood back behind the house as if they were scared to death of us, but once the captain warmed up to us, the others started coming out. We weren't going to ask to sleep there unless they asked us. The experiences that Fred had in August were still fresh in our minds as well as these villagers refusing to allow Allie Lee and Kathy to sleep there. We were very surprised when the captain invited us to stay, even though 100 people were living in the same long house. We also had butterflies in our stomachs, as we feared they might have menacing plans for us.

As the evening progressed the villagers became friendlier. The captain gave us casaba (a bread-like substance made from grated yuca root), bananas and pineapple. The captain then asked us for some of our own bread, so we gave him some that we had brought for our lunch. This was an encouraging sign. He also asked our doctor to put medicine on a sore on his leg which demonstrated trust. Once the others saw the captain do this, they asked for medicine. Just several days previously, they wouldn't accept medicine.

Move into Parguaza River Area

We left Bonafacios' village around 9:00 a.m. the next morning. Once we got back to the boat, we went down river and found a nice place to stop and cook breakfast. After we cooked breakfast, we went on our way down river to Pendare. We had lots of fun coming back down through the rapids. We visited the villages again as we came down river, and the doctor treated those that were sick. We were tired and sunburned when we arrived home, but it was good be back and see the kids again even though it had only been one night. Our little hut in Pendare looked like a mansion compared to where we had spent the night before.

Before the doctor and his wife left, he requested to visit Caño Piapoco which was where the villagers had wanted to kill Fred and Santiago during their initial visit the previous August. This was the first time Fred had returned to that village. The villagers were friendly but still did not want anyone to teach them about God.

As news of our presence, medicine and teaching spread up and down the river, many from other villages moved to Pendare where they could learn to read, hear about a living God, and receive medicine. The village of 30 grew to more than 300 within a couple of years.

In the beginning, as we were teaching them day after day, there were many times we had to encourage them to go home and get some sleep as we needed it also. In these earlier teaching sessions, we always began with the creation story and worked our way through the Old Testament laying a foundation of who God is. Then we would present the birth, death and resurrection of Jesus Christ, and the reason for His coming.

Journey into the Unknown

During this time, a young boy, about seven or eight years old, was bitten by a poisonous snake. The witchdoctor came to Fred and told him, "My specialty in witchcraft is snake bites and people do not die when I treat them, but this time I am not going to do anything as I want to see if your God is stronger than my witchcraft." This was quite a challenge, and we told him that it is not always God's wish for the person not to die, but we accepted the challenge. We gave the boy a pre-anti-venom test to see if he was allergic before giving the full treatment. The place on his wrist where the test was given immediately swelled up showing that he was very allergic to it and could die from the medicine. We prayed and asked God for wisdom and His intervention. Our faith was tested once again as we felt we should give him the full treatment. The people witnessed us praying to our God. God showed His power and the next day the boy was running and playing as if nothing had happened.

The witchdoctor came by later and said that they wanted to believe in our God. We had already taught them about the concept of God and things related to the birth of Jesus Christ. However, we also wanted them to know the power that He has compared to their tribal beliefs and their witchdoctor. In their wanting to believe in our God, they had to understand that this was a personal commitment between them and God. We explained about Jesus' birth, His life, His death, and His resurrection. We explained to them that only in believing that Jesus died and rose again for their sins would they have forgiveness of their sins and become true believers in God.

Move into Parguaza River Area

We will never forget that evening. Our small living room was full of people sitting on the benches around the walls and on the floor in the middle of the room. After their hearing about our true God, many villagers accepted Jesus as their Savior. We talked to each of them individually to make sure they understood. They were so hungry to know God's Word that they stayed there day and night asking questions and wanting to hear more. I marveled and was thrilled that I had witnessed many receive the greatest gift of all: God's love to the World. I wanted to find a way to remember this date. I looked at the calendar, and it was February 14, Valentine's Day.

Melanie & Brian with Children

We noticed an increased desire from the villagers to learn to read so they could understand more about God's Word. We had never seen so much enthusiasm. We had a full morning and afternoon of literacy classes with them. The evening was dedicated to teaching them God's Word. Even with all this, if there was any time in between, they were in our house with their papers asking us to listen to them read their vowels. Even their children were eager to learn. They wanted Melanie to listen to them read the paper with the syllables on them, which she did with the moral support of her little brother sitting beside her on a log outside.

Another thing that filled our hearts with joy was seeing their desire to do what the Lord would have them do. One

Journey into the Unknown

of the hardest things for them was to give up the dope, the chanting to evil spirits, and the charms that were central to their traditional belief system. We saw them, of their own volition, get rid of these things and declare their faith in God and not in witchcraft.

We know that when God is working, Satan will not easily give up his battle to defeat God's work. We saw this so many times on the Parguaza River where Satan had free reign for so many years and successfully put fear and lies in the minds of the people. He used the witchdoctors to spread the word of the missionaries' arrival, and the evil things he claimed we would do. One of the lies concerned the house we built in their village. We had a big hole at the side of the house where we had dug dirt to build the mud walls. The witchdoctor told the people that the hole was where we would bury the bones of their children after we killed and ate them.

The influence of the witchdoctors was great, and their involvement in every aspect of the villages culture was enormous. After becoming believers, the Piaroas would often be concerned about what to do when they became sick or were bitten by a snake. Now that they were Christians, they understood that they could not go to the witchdoctors for chanting. We encouraged them to pray and ask God's protection and assured them that we would be praying for them also. Gonzalos' face lit up after hearing this, and he said, "God is stronger than the devil, isn't He? We will talk to Him."

The Lord blessed our time in the Parguaza River as many made professions of faith in the Lord in the two villages in which we and our co-workers lived. One of our last

Move into Parguaza River Area

Sundays there, we had a baptismal service and 41 testified of faith in their Lord and Savior. To them, this was something new as they had never seen a baptismal service but were very happy because they were learning new truths and following the Lord. The house was full for the service, and they all sang with much enthusiasm. Chief Prinio's face was all aglow as he listened to the message. When Fred gave the villagers an opportunity to give their testimonies, Chief Prinio said, "I am not bathing [getting baptized] today, I am sick." After some of the others gave their testimonies, the chief found the courage to give his testimony and was baptized. He was happy again and encouraged his wife to give hers.

During a later visit, there were 32 new believers baptized. Among them was another witchdoctor who was an old, grey headed grandpa. They named him Adam as he had gray hair and that was rarely seen among the Piaroas. He took his stand for the Lord. Afterwards, he went back to his house and brought out a little basket with his witchcraft implements. While he slowly threw them one by one into the river, he gave his testimony to over 200 bystanders. Several hundred more would hear about it later. He now trusted in a greater power, the God of the universe. It took great faith in God to turn his back on the only security he had ever known. A witchdoctor depends on the implements of his profession to protect him from all harm. It brought tears to our eyes to witness what God had done in the hearts of the people on the Parguaza River.

Many villages were still afraid and were waiting to see what was going to happen to those that were turning from their old ways and learning "the Book." The last week we

Journey into the Unknown

were there, two chiefs from different villages came out with a group to ask questions. Chief Bonifacio came down and wanted to talk with Fred. Bonifacio told Fred that the next year his people wanted to move down below the rapids and build a new village, so they could learn about God. As we were in the canoe leaving, he came running down the river bank and called us to come back as he had a couple more questions for Fred. He wanted to know when the Lord Jesus was coming again, and if He would be coming before he could learn and be saved. On that trip, he did not accept the Lord. However, on a return trip to that area, we saw Bonifacio put his faith in the Lord Jesus Christ and accept Him as his Savior. As a testimony to his new faith, he returned to his house, gathered up all of his witchcraft paraphernalia, and threw them in the river. It was one of the highlights of our time there.

With more missionaries entering the mission field, the work continued to grow to more villages. We were continually blessed when we heard how the Gospel was spreading. As we look back on what God did on the Parguaza, this verse became our prayer.

"Being confident of this very thing, that He which hath begun a good work in you will perform it until the day of Jesus Christ." Philippians 1:6

Journey into the Unknown

Chapter 15 – Back to San Juan

"For we wrestle not against flesh and blood, but against principalities and powers, against the rulers of the darkness of this world, against spiritual wickedness in high places." Ephesians 6:12

We had to cut our time short in the Parguaza River area due to a medical problem with Melanie. We noticed that she wanted to sleep a lot without the desire to eat and to play. Being far from any doctor, we used our limited medical knowledge and concluded that she might have either malaria or hepatitis. We took her out to Puerto Ayacucho where she was checked by a doctor and hospitalized for tests. They confirmed that she had type B hepatitis which was contagious. They said she had probably been contaminated from an infected needle.

We struggled to think of how that had happened. Then we remembered that a few months ago, Melanie was punctured in the leg by a rusty nail while playing. We took her to the local hospital for a tetanus shot. We later learned that many times the needles were used on other people and then reused without proper sterilization. At that time, there were several patients in the hospital with hepatitis when she received the shot. So, we were pretty sure that is where she was infected.

The doctor confirmed Melanie had hepatitis. He said he could not properly treat her there and we needed to take her to the best children's hospital in Caracas. She was hospitalized for eight days and diagnosed with prolonged hepatitis. Her liver and spleen were both enlarged from it.

Back to San Juan

Meanwhile, Brian became sick with malaria while his Grandma was keeping him in Puerto Ayacucho, and we asked her to bring him to Caracas also to be examined. The doctor discovered the initial signs of hepatitis B in him as well. He received treatment before it advanced. This was just another bump in the road, but once again we thank the Lord for His loving care for us and our children.

After a follow-up trip to Caracas to have Melanie checked again for hepatitis, she was given a clean bill of health by the doctor. So, we returned to San Juan. Our desire was to get involved again in teaching the new believers and discipling the church leaders in San Juan. We also made plans for seminars in the villages where there were new church plants. During this time, I taught Melanie using a kindergarten correspondence course that was sent to us from the U.S. I enjoyed teaching her, especially since I knew that it would only be for a few years before she would need a more qualified teacher. This would mean sending her to the TamaTama missionary children's school. Fortunately, Melanie and I finished the Kindergarten course before our next unexpected move.

We received a letter from the field leadership asking if we would move to TamaTama for a year to fill vacancies. Our beloved founder and chairman, Robert Shaylor, had passed away from hepatitis a couple of years earlier. We filled in until the newly appointed chairman, Paul Dye, returned from home assignment.

While in TamaTama, the school year commenced for the missionary children. We were fortunate that we worked on the school base during Melanie's first year there. Being so close to school worked out great, until one day Melanie's

Journey into the Unknown

little brother decided he missed his big sister. Unbeknownst to me, he decided to slip out of the house and follow her to school. She was not aware of it until she arrived at school, and then had to bring him back home. That made her late for school, and she was scolded for it. This was only her first week of school and she came home in tears.

Aerial View of TamaTama

Our job there was to oversee the base, meet the visitors coming through, and help with entertaining. It was during this time that we experienced many frustrating government and military investigations. For many years, false rumors had been circulating through the country concerning our mission and what we were doing in the jungles isolated from civilization. Many people wondered why Americans and other foreigners were willing to live in such isolation and have their young children grow up there without all the comforts and safety of their home country. This idea became a tool in the minds of the leftist groups and enemies of the Gospel and contributed to more false rumors. We were accused of changing the culture of the people and extracting their natural resources for personal gain.

One rumor claimed we had clandestine airstrips in isolated places that could not be seen from the air. According to the rumor, our small one engine mission plane left the States loaded with arms and ammunition for us to give to people so they (and we) could take over the country. When the little plane was near the base where the missionaries were, the pilot would push a button on the control panel of the plane and the jungle would open. The pilot could then land on a hidden airstrip, unload the arms, and at the same time pick up the missionaries' dirty laundry. The dirty laundry would be taken back to the States to be laundered and brought back to them on the next trip along with more arms and ammunition. After the pilot took off with the dirty laundry, he would push the button again, and the airstrip would once again be covered up by the jungle.

These and many more false accusations drew the attention of the government and military leaders. That is why different groups of investigators visited the mission bases and questioned us as well as anyone who knew us. Ironically, the missionaries had been requesting for quite some time that the government and military officials come down and see for themselves what we were doing. We knew we had nothing to hide and the rumors were false, so we were glad that these investigations happened. Many times, Fred was asked to accompany them as they visited villages. They wanted all their conversations recorded, so Fred would hold the tape recorder, and translate, as they asked questions. One night when they were all sleeping in hammocks in a mission house, the main investigator jumped out of his hammock in the middle of the night and loudly proclaimed so that all could hear, "I know! I know what the problem is with New Tribes Mission! It is because you are a group of foreigners down here in the jungles and there are no Venezuelan nationals working with you."

Journey into the Unknown

This struck a chord with us as we had already been talking about the need to prepare Venezuelans to work beside us as missionaries. Our goal as missionaries was to prepare faithful Venezuelan men to take over the work we were doing. In other words, "work ourselves out of a job." Not only was it our desire to see this, but also to prepare them to continue the work as we did not know how much longer we could stay in the country. During this time our mission went through a difficult time getting visas for new missionaries to join us, and we lost some of our present staff to sicknesses and death. We knew that we as a family could not get involved in this until after we finished the translation of the New Testament in the Piaroa language. However, the desire to prepare Venezuelans to become missionaries became a burden on our hearts. We prayed to be a part of this.

"And the things that thou hast heard of me among many witnesses, the same commit thou to faithful men, who shall be able to teach others also." 2 Timothy 2:2

As time went on, we continued to experience growing opposition against our work. The name for New Tribes Mission in Spanish is 'Nuevas Tribus' and the word for oust is "Fuera." "Fuera Nuevas Tribus" was seen written on walls, on signs, and even on big rocks located along the side of the roads. NTM continued to reach out to as many tribes as possible. We continued teaching, church planting, and translating knowing we might have to leave at any time due to opposition. We tried to keep a low profile, but it was difficult as we were foreigners. Thanks to many prayers from all over the world, the Lord was not through with us yet.

Back to San Juan

Melanie in Front Left

After Melanie finished the first grade, we returned to San Juan for a short time. During this time, I experienced the hardest part of foreign missionary work, separation from my children. We sent our little seven-year-old girl off to a missionary boarding school. Even though we knew it was best for her, it still tore at our hearts. We walked her to the airstrip and tried to be positive and brave as she left on the MAF plane for a two-hour flight to TamaTama. After the plane left and we were alone, we broke out in tears. Even though it was hard, we were thankful for the dedicated missionary teachers and dorm parents who cared for our children. The first time Melanie went to school, it was 11 weeks before she had a two week break and came home. How we looked forward to her two weeks at home, but always in the back of our minds was the thought that we would be sending her off again. It never seemed any easier even once the separation time was reduced to eight weeks.

In between our moves from one place to another, we continued to have a ministry with the Piaroas in San Juan as well as the Spanish speaking population in San Juan which had grown quite a bit. Fred developed many good friendships and participated in community sports and games. We started inviting people to our house on Saturday nights to enjoy refreshments while playing games and studying the Bible. This took on the name "Evangelical Club." In the beginning, only five came and then it grew to

Journey into the Unknown

12. There were many that wanted to come, but they were afraid of the word "evangelical."

As time passed, more and more people from surrounding areas came to San Juan and heard the Word of God many for the first time. In this group were also some national guards that we became close friends with. Several accepted the Lord and all of them heard the Gospel. When we had to leave San Juan for a period, the missionaries that stayed there continued to carry on this ministry. We would later receive letters telling us how God had blessed them.

On one occasion, missionaries from the Orinoco River Mission, who worked mainly with Spanish speaking people, offered to hold an evangelical outreach in San Juan. They had a lot of experience working with national people. Two families, the Glen Irwins and the Barclay Harleys, came for the outreach. The small San Juan church could not accommodate a large crowd, so we held the outreach outside. The Irwins and Harleys showed some Christian movies with a clear message of salvation. They also preached afterwards. We did not have electricity, except for a small generator, because the town generator was out of fuel. For the screen, we put two poles in the ground with a white sheet tied between them, and we placed speakers on each side of the screen. Thanks to having a small generator we were quite an attraction in a place where there were no other lights, television, or radio. The crowds came from all over.

These open-air meetings proved to be a rich, spiritual blessing. Many people received the Lord as their personal Savior, including a group of Piaroas who for years lived in their own community in San Juan. This group of Piaroas

Back to San Juan

were previously antagonistic to the gospel, opposed Christians, and went so far as to burn the translated New Testament books of their relatives. Others, who had fallen out of fellowship with the Lord for years, were restored to fellowship.

The day following the close of the evangelical outreach was a Sunday. The crowd was too big to fit in the little church, so the service was again held in the open air with benches set under the trees. After the morning service, we gathered at the river for a baptismal service in which around 65 were baptized. It was a time of great joy as we witnessed the work of the Lord in our midst.

In the days and weeks following, the Lord continued to work in hearts and the little church was packed out on Sundays. Plans for a larger church building had already been in process and the initial groundwork started. Plans had been made with the Orinoco River Mission to have another evangelistic outreach the next year. It would be rainy season, and we knew we would need a larger church to hold the meetings inside. The Piaroas were enthused about building a larger church especially one made with cement blocks that would last a long time. This took almost a year as they did most of the work with many delays due to finances and opposition. However, there was an unfinished building with a roof on it for the second outreach. This time a Venezuelan pastor from Ciudad Bolivar along with another missionary, John Prince from the Orinoco River Mission, came along with other missionaries from NTM. It only rained one day, but the crowds were larger than the first one. This church, which seated 300, was overflowing to the point many Piaroas

Journey into the Unknown

were looking through the windows. Missionary participants estimated that there were around 600 that heard the message during the week-long outreach. Many made professions of faith.

After this, a small radio station was installed in the area through a government contract. The owners of the radio station offered NTM a spot on the radio each day, as they had done for the Catholic mission. Through the Orinoco River Mission, we provided Christian programs on tape for the radio station. One tape was a devotional called "Ecos del Cielo" (Echos from Heaven) and another one was called "Unshackled." Later, they allowed us to air a program for children on Saturdays despite efforts to block these programs.

Journey into the Unknown

Chapter 16 - Troubling Times

In 1976, having just returned from home assignment, we were asked to fill in for our Field Administrator, Don Bodin in Puerto Ayacucho while they were in the States on home assignment. This was one of several times that we filled this position. The first time was the hardest as there was so much to learn. After 17 years living with a tribe and translating, we now had to transition as an accountant along with other additional leadership responsibilities!

Meanwhile, the continued false accusations and lies against NTM mounted. More investigating committees appointed by the president came through with their body guards. They once again requested that Fred accompany them on the trips they made to the different tribal bases. After one trip in which they saw the results of the Gospel changing lives, they wrote up a very positive report about NTM that contained this statement: "We have seen the 'diamonds' they are extracting." They were referring to the newly converted souls. The investigators told us that even though their report was very positive, there were still many in the Capitol that wanted us out of the country and were trying to find something against us.

When the Bodins returned from home assignment a year later, we were able to move back to the tribe we had been missing. Before returning to San Juan, Fred was asked by the field leadership if he would go with Don Bodin to a little town of San Fernando de Apure, an hour's flight from Ayacucho. This is where the new missionaries studied Spanish before moving on to their assignment. We started getting visas for new missionaries who were arriving to

Troubling Times

start their Spanish course. Fred and Don went to meet them and go over field policies and orientation with them. They were able to answer any questions the new missionaries had to make the transition easier.

By this time, both of our children were of school age and were at our NTM missionaries' children's school in TamaTama. I was still in Puerto Ayacucho waiting for Fred to return. While Fred was on this trip, two National Guards came to our NTM headquarters asking for the person in charge. Since Fred was still in that position, they wanted to talk to him. I explained to them that he was in San Fernando de Apure but should fly back the next day. They accepted that explanation and left. A couple hours later, they came back and asked to talk to me. They told me that since my husband was not there, they wanted me to go with them to the guards' station. I knew I had to go but asked them if I could take someone else with me. They agreed. The first missionary I saw was Wally Jank, who was also a member of the field leadership team. I asked him if he would go with me. We climbed in the back of the guards' Jeep and were taken down to their station. We later found out that it was illegal for them to take another member of the family in for questioning instead of the one they were seeking, but we didn't know that then.

When we got to the station, they told us that they were going to question us and to sit in chairs outside their office. They later came out and asked who wanted to go first. Wally spoke up quickly and said, "I will." As I was sitting there alone, a guard recognized me. He had been stationed in San Juan and attended the Bible Club that we had in our home for Spanish speaking nationals. He also knew Fred

Journey into the Unknown

from when he first arrived in Venezuela as a MK; they used to play marbles and other games together during those early years. He came over and sat by me and asked what I was doing there. I told him that I really didn't know. I explained they came looking for Fred, but since he was out of town they asked me to come with them. He asked me if I was scared. I told him I was, and that I did not know what this was all about. Furthermore, I wondered what questions they were going to ask me and if I would know the answers. I was afraid I would not understand the questions and because of my misunderstanding, my answers might somehow incriminate my husband and NTM. He seemed to understand and excused himself to go talk with another guard. I don't know what they talked about, but he came back to me with the other guard who tried to talk to me in English. I didn't understand anything he was saying. After they talked to each other, the guard that I knew came back to me and the only thing he said was, "go with this guard." I didn't ask any questions but followed him out of the building and climbed into the back of the Jeep again. He drove me to the front of our mission headquarters and stopped. When I asked if I could go now, he said I could. Wally, unfortunately, was not as lucky. He was taken straight to jail after they finished questioning him.

I composed myself and told the others what had happened, then called Fred in San Fernando de Apure and told him about it. I warned him the guards would probably be at the airport waiting for him when he came in the next day. I was so thankful that Melanie and Brian were in TamaTama and were not there during this time. Wally and his two younger children were in Puerto Ayacucho doing paperwork as they were on their way to Canada to be with his wife, Marg. She

Troubling Times

was there for an extended time for medical care. While he took my place and went to jail, I took care of his children. This was good for me as it kept my mind off what was happening. Wally was relieved, as he knew someone was taking care of his children.

The next day when Don and Fred arrived at the airport, they were met by the guards. They were asked one question, "Do you know Larry Bockus?" Don could honestly answer "no" as Larry and his family had arrived while Don was away on home assignment. Fred, however, did know Larry and had to answer "yes." Fred had met them when they came through Puerto Ayacucho on their way to San Juan to be part of the Piaroa team. Don was told by the guards that he could leave, but they took Fred with them for questioning to the jail where Wally had already been taken. Fred and Wally soon learned the reason they were detained. It was another trumped-up effort to find NTM guilty of something, so they could kick us out of the country. They thought they had finally found the proof they needed.

The reason they asked the men if they knew Larry was because when his belongings arrived from the States, the guards found used military apparel. Since the uniforms were made of good quality material and Larry was going to be living and working in the jungles, Larry thought this type of clothing would be very useful to him. However, when the guards saw the uniforms and discovered that he was a Vietnam veteran of high rank, they feared he was going to start a rebellion through our mission. Even worse, we were unaware there was a law against bringing foreign military uniforms into the country. The guards immediately

Journey into the Unknown

came to our headquarters and asked for Larry. Since Larry was not there, they asked for the one in charge, and that was Fred. This was normal procedure; the person in charge is held responsible for the one under him if he is guilty of breaking the law.

Since Larry was the main reason for the arrests, they could not proceed with the investigation until they could get him out from the jungle base to the town where Fred and Wally remained detained. Fred and Wally, even though in jail, had special privileges since Fred knew the governor and other high-ranking policemen. Instead of sleeping in a cell, they slept in the police officers' bedroom and were the recipients of many other freedoms on the condition they didn't leave the jail. Our mission plane was the only one available at that time, so we offered to fly Larry in from San Juan. Upon his arrival in Puerto Ayacucho, he was taken straight to jail where Fred and Wally were. They put him in a crowded cell with the other criminals where he could have no contact with the other two. We often talked about how the one most prepared to be in that place was Larry, since he had been a Ranger in the Vietnam war.

During this time, we heard conflicting stories about what was being done to resolve the situation. Fred and Wally were told one thing, and we on the outside were told something different. Fortunately, Don had immediately called the American Embassy, the Venezuelan government, and military officials he knew to let them know what was happening. I received calls from people in high government positions within an hour of Don's phone call, one of which was a leading candidate for the presidential election (later he won the presidency). Also, we received calls from a

Troubling Times

Venezuelan senator whom Fred had accompanied on one of the investigations and the General Secretary of the same political party. They all confirmed that this was an injustice and the charges against us were trumped up. They went to work immediately to try to free Fred, Wally, and Larry.

The day after Larry arrived, the three of them were sent to Caracas on a commercial airline to a military criminal court. They decided amongst themselves that they wanted to dress up rather than wear their dirty, smelly, jail clothes as they were not criminals and did not want to appear as such. They were escorted by military guards and seated in the front of the plane with the guards behind them. No one could tell that they were being taken to prison. They appeared to be important people escorted by the guards. Upon their arrival in Caracas, they were taken to the worst prison in the country where the worst of the criminals were. Many times guards used torture in this prison to extract confessions from prisoners. God in His mercy kept all of us from knowing this until after the fact.

Our Field Chairman, another couple and I were flown by the MAF plane to a small airport on the outskirts of Caracas. When we arrived at our mission apartment in Caracas, our field chairman started calling the government officials that he and Fred had contacts with to find out what was happening. One Venezuelan senator told the chairman that he was calling the military officials' office every 15 minutes and was keeping after them until they released the three men. The military officials promised us that the men would be freed before nightfall.

When they were released, and I saw Fred again, he told us what happened when they were in jail in Caracas. The first night, they were put in individual 7' X 9' cells next to each other where they could talk. On the second night after they had been interrogated for several hours, they accepted the fact that they would be spending yet another night in prison. Suddenly, they heard a lot of noise like doors and chains rattling. Then the guards came to the cell doors of the three men and opened them up. The guards told them to "get out of there." They were quickly out on the street. You can only imagine the joy we felt when the three men walked through the doorway of the mission apartment.

After the three men were released, each one returned to the place of their previous ministries. We returned to Puerto Ayacucho to finish packing for San Juan. Our equipment for San Juan (that we had brought back from home assignment a year and a half earlier) was still in Puerto Ayacucho in 50-gallon barrels. We felt it would be a good idea to go through the barrels before shipping them just in case there might be something that could be used to incriminate us. We thank the Lord for bringing this to our attention as we found several green, military duffle bags that we had bought from an Army surplus store. These bags were strong and durable and very useful to carry hammocks, mosquito nets, river and hiking clothes in for traveling. These were so valuable living in the jungles, and we had several of these in the barrels. To use them without getting in trouble, we dyed them black. We never had any trouble with them after that!

While our barrels were waiting at the port to be loaded on the boat, some guards came up and asked to search them. The owner of the boat watched as they went through our things. One guard got real excited as he took out a box

Troubling Times

from one of our barrels. He held up a small book of instructions in English and yelled loudly, "I found it, I found it!" When the owner of the boat asked him what he found, he replied, "I found their plans for taking over the country." He was very excited that he had it in his hands. The owner of the boat started laughing at him. He told him, "you have the instructions for a child's erector set (Tinker Toys)." He had found instructions for Brian's birthday present. The guard was not convinced until the boat owner explained it to him. We can laugh at some of these things now, but at that time it was not a laughing matter. Soon after this, we were finally on our way back home to San Juan.

We felt that when we got back to our home in the jungles, we would be out of the spotlight and free of the harassment. It was not like that. Although there were no more jail experiences, we did have some scares. A few months after our return, guards arrived at our house with a citation for Fred to appear at their office. This time, the situation was resolved without consequence (jail time). However, it left us weak and fearful, especially if a strange plane would fly over or a national guard would come to our door. Fear from this and the struggles we continued to have finishing the New Testament were wearing on us. Several years later we noticed that when one of us would go through times of discouragement and be ready to give up, the other one would be strong and encouraging. During these times, we would ask ourselves, "why did we come and what was our commitment to the Lord?" When we thought about the answer to those two questions, we could not give up.

Journey into the Unknown

Several years later, we were asked again to return to Puerto Ayacucho to fill in for the administrator. When we left San Juan this time, we had a feeling we would not be going back. Part of the roof of our house was falling in due to termites. We also had other co-workers who could continue the ministry. The accusations against NTM continued. Several of our missionaries spent time in jail.

Two of our substitute high school teachers were jailed and had to leave the country. Once they left, the high school students had to be home schooled or sent to another mission school in a city far from us. Melanie, a senior, was blessed to have a former teacher/principal in our midst. The wife of one of the pilots offered to finish teaching the high school students that year. The following year, Brian and several others transferred to Christiansen Academy located in a town on the western side of Venezuela where they eventually graduated from high school.

Another attempt made against NTM was to get signatures from people of the different tribes we were working with. They deceived the villagers by telling them that if they signed their names to a list, they would get free meals in one of the schools. They didn't realize that they were signing a petition to have us thrown out of the country. The signatures of the tribal people were valuable as ammunition against us.

The opposition passed around banners and posters to have us ousted. People walked up and down the streets with big banners that said NTM should leave. One such poster said that we would be thrown out of the country on March 26th, but it didn't happen. They even wrote on rocks and some of the walls that NTM should be ousted from Venezuela.

Troubling Times

We received word there was going to be a huge demonstration on May 1st against NTM. May 1st was the day they celebrated the Day of the Workers (like the U.S. Labor Day). We feared it would become violent and were advised to leave town and move the airplanes to a safe place. We decided on a place to go and prepared food and supplies we might need to take. Meanwhile, back in the States, my parents had heard about the situation and had sent an urgent letter requesting prayer to all our supporters, other churches, and people in foreign countries that knew us. May 1st arrived, and it was a Sunday morning. We woke up in the early morning to the sound of thunder and heavy rain. It was intense, and the rain did not let up until afternoon, so no one dared go out in the streets. No one came out to demonstrate against us or damage our planes due to this very unusual storm! We gathered together later that day and held a prayer and praise service. One of the songs we sang was, "There shall be showers of blessings."

As we reflected upon this time, a verse came back to us that a Venezuelan Christian lady sent to us:

"The Lord will fight for you and you shall hold your peace." Exodus 14:14.

Chapter 17 – Translation

"The entrance of Your Word gives light; It gives understanding to the simple." Psalm 119:130

During our missionary training with NTM, we were taught methods for learning languages and cultures with the goal of not only speaking the language but developing an alphabet. Once an alphabet was established, it was possible to create literacy primers to teach villagers how to read in their own language. Then Bible stories would be translated for more reading material. When we went to Venezuela, we worked with a people group just like that, the Piaroas. Though their language was rich in vocabulary and grammar, they had no alphabet or written form.

To translate the Bible, we needed to accurately portray the truths of scripture in a language and culture that had no concept of the true creator and God. We also needed to not just learn their language, but to learn it fluently. Additionally, we needed to learn their culture in depth, their religious beliefs, and what motivated and dominated their ways of thinking. With all this information, we started to create a translation they could understand.

The first missionaries to learn the Piaroa language started in the early 50's. Mary Lou Yount and Fred were pioneers in this endeavor. No outsider spoke the Piaroa language before that. Very few Piaroas could speak any Spanish at all which meant there was no common language to start from. To learn their language, Fred pointed to an object and the Piaroa told him what it was called. This went on for several hours as Fred wrote down what he thought he

Translation

heard. When he grew tired or ran out of time, he went home and memorized these words, so that in his next session he could say a few of them. However, things were not so simple. The next day, he went to the same person and pointed to the same object and repeated the word he had learned, that person shook his head and said a different word. Fred was puzzled but wrote down the new word and continued his studies. The next day, he tried out his new word, and the native shook his head yet again and said a third word. By this time, Fred was baffled. He put a big question mark by the word and continued on to a new word. As many months passed, and he learned more of the language, he finally realized what was happening. The first word given was a generic word for the item, for example, wood. The second word was a more precise word, meaning tree. The third word was the exact kind of tree, a mango tree. Such was the repetitive process of the language learning phase. It seemed like a never-ending endeavor, but eventually Fred and Mary Lou began to understand the intricacies of the language and formed a Piaroa alphabet for the first time in history.

While learning words, phrases and sentences, another problem arose: numbers and counting. In the Piaroa language there is not just one word for "one" or "two" or "three," but many ways of saying each number up to the number twenty. Beyond twenty, two hands (5 fingers each hand) and two feet (5 toes to each foot) everything just becomes "many." As we tried to get words for numbers, we learned that each object, depending on its size and shape, was a different word. To say one round rubber ball, we would have to say, "one small, round, rubber object." To say five round rubber balls, we would have to say, "one

Journey into the Unknown

hand of small, round, rubber objects." If we had 12 round rubber balls, we would have to say, "two hands and two toes of small, round, rubber objects" and so on. As you can see, this became very complicated, so we opted to teach the numbers in Spanish and use the Spanish numbering system.

Also, the language had 27 consonants and included three t's, three p's and three c's each with a different sound. We had the regular t (t), the aspirated t (tt) and the glottal t ('t). The incorrect use of these consonants could change the meaning of the word. One instance was the word cuiti. Cuiti with a regular t, meant "eat it" and cuįttį, with an aspirated t, meant "your son." The language also had seven vowels. The same seven vowels with a nasal tone made a total of 14 different vowel sounds. All these intricacies added to the difficulty of learning to speak and put in to writing this language.

As we were mastering the language, we were also learning the culture of the people. Without knowing the culture, we would not have been able to do any effective teaching or Bible translation. We had to know how they thought, why they thought that way, and how to communicate with them outside of our own way of thinking. We also needed to know what, how, and why they believed what they believed. For instance, having a "change of heart" had no meaning whatsoever to them. Some tribes only understood it when it was translated "a change of liver." Thus, it was important to both learn the language and culture fluently.

The first translated material done by Fred was in 1960, and that was a book of Old Testament stories and some key scripture verses. He also translated the book of Mark, which was the first book of the Bible to be translated. The

Translation

last book of the New Testament translated was Revelation in 1974. Then, we had to revise the translation, as over time, Fred and Mary Lou learned new words and better ways of translating. This eventually required another complete revision and typing before the New Testament could be sent to the printer. Why did it take so many years? I am glad you asked. When we were working in a tribe of people, there were many unexpected situations that kept us from reaching our goals. There were times when we found ourselves alone with the tribe as there always seemed to be a shortage of co-workers. During those times, translation was given a back seat. When we had co-workers, many times they became sick and had to leave for medical help. Other co-workers had to leave for much needed home assignment time. Many times, there were needs in other areas of the tribe where people were begging for a missionary to come and teach them. How could we say "no, we can't go?" We either sent a co-worker, if we had one, or we put on hold our present ministry and went ourselves.

One time, we tried to start a new mission base and continue to translate at the same time. So, we settled in a new village and a small palm house on the Parguaza River. We had one table made of a split palm tree. This was the only table in the house and was used for preparing meals, eating, and translating. Fred would open all the books that he used in translating and leave a space to do the writing. When the Piaroas entered our house and saw books for the first time, they wanted to know what all the marks on the pages were! They would pick up the reference books and Bibles and would go through them. Unfortunately, Fred had left them at specific pages for his research and translation. Once the Piaroas went through the books, the place where Fred left

Journey into the Unknown

off was lost. Also, they had never seen a pencil before. They were full of questions about the pencils and picked them up for a closer look. After a couple days of trying to translate under these conditions, we decided that this was not the time or place to do translation. There were other things more pressing. Thus, we encountered another long delay in translating.

The place and time we lived in when we were involved in translation was so different than it would be today. We lived in the southern part of Venezuela and out of reach of many conveniences that we were accustomed to in the States. We had no electricity in the tropical temperature that reached often reached 120 degrees in the shade of our front porch. I typed on an old Smith-Corona, non-electric typewriter. Due to the language alphabet, special keys were adapted on the typewriter. This was before computers and copying machines. To make copies of the typed manuscripts, we used carbon paper. We typed four to five copies at one time. The translation helpers took them home to read. The following day they came back with any questions about what they could not understand or with a better way to say it. We also checked for spelling and typographical errors. To correct a mistake, we often had to re-type an entire page again and again until no mistakes appeared in retyping.

Even though other ministry needs understandably became priorities, finishing the New Testament weighed heavily on our hearts. We, along with our field leadership, felt that we needed to go to an isolated place where we could focus on translation full-time. They suggested we go to one of the tribes where we could not speak their language, a non-

Translation

Piaroa tribe where they didn't know us and what we were doing. A tribe with other missionaries that treated the sick, taught the language, and cared for the people, thus allowing us to focus intently on translation. This also required a house for us to live in. Remember the village where the airplane dropped in supplies because they were isolated? The Blincos started working in Caño Iguana the year before, and another family joined them. As God's timing is always perfect, one of the families had to leave for home assignment, and their house was available for us to use. We decided to go there for two months and then return to San Juan. We took a Piaroa family with us to help free up more of our time. Among the many things they did was make a bed out of poles and vines for Brian, who was still at home, helped clean the house, washed dishes, washed clothes, etc. Now, we could dedicate our time to translating.

Translating the New Testament

The first day Fred started translating we had company! How was that possible? The only way to get there was by flying on the small mission plane which did not come in that day. The villagers told us about these visitors. They said they were white like us and could not speak their language. Fred went out and saw that they were the anthropologists that had come to our house in San Juan before we left. The other missionary wife working with this tribe, Harriet Kennedy, and I prepared a fast meal for them. They were supposed to go to a different Yuana village but ended up where we were. They had walked several days just to find out they were at the wrong place. Fred encouraged them to go back to San Juan to get carriers and guides to help them get where they planned to go. They left shortly after dinner. We later laughed that we thought we were in a place where we would have no interruptions!

As soon as Fred had a chapter finished, I typed up the manuscript. The Piaroa, that came along to help us, could read, so he told us if something didn't make sense. This was helpful, but we still needed a translator helper to work with Fred. After a couple of weeks, we received good news by radio that Rafael Perez was coming to work with Fred. Rafael was the captain of the Piaroas in San Juan, a church leader, and a translator helper for much of the translation already finished. This was another answer to prayer.

Typing the New Testament

Rafael had been sick for some time, and after a recent check-up he was diagnosed with tuberculosis. We did not know if it was chronic or contagious. Fred and I both had the tuberculosis vaccine, but Brian had not had it yet. We had been trying for some time to get Brian vaccinated, because tuberculosis was prevalent among the Piaroas. We received an answer to prayer with having an experienced translator helper, yet at the same time, we felt a certain amount of fear due to exposing our son and others living there to tuberculosis. We prayed about this, and I decided to keep his dishes separate from ours. I did not want him to feel embarrassed, so I came up with the idea of putting a red dot on the bottom of the tin plates, glasses and silverware he used. I always washed them with scalding water. I was satisfied that it was working, and that he didn't notice the difference. One day as we sat down at the table to eat, I saw him lift his plate and glass to look for the red dot. So much for that idea! After a few months we returned to San Juan and continued working there.

The first draft of the New Testament was finished in 1974. It had been over 14 years in the making. We were thankful that the books could be printed (mimeographed) in our small print shop in Puerto Ayacucho and passed out to the people as each book of the Bible was translated. This enabled the missionaries to continue teaching from God's Word as well as help catch any mistakes or misunderstandings. The next step was a complete revision of the New Testament before sending it to the printer. This needed to be done since it had been so many years since the first verse was translated.

In 1976, we started the revision process of our first draft which took several years. We found bilingual Piaroas from different areas of the tribe to help with this revision.

Revising the New Testament

Fred and Mary Lou Yount were weary from working a long and hard time on this, but the Piaroas who helped were impacted even more as they were not used to sitting inside

Journey into the Unknown

for hours around a long table. Their lives had been about fishing and hunting out in the jungle before they volunteered to help translate. They met together on our front porch in the heat. We had no electricity, so a fan was useless. This revision did not take as long as the initial translation, but there were many delays like home assignments and unexpected medical problems.

One such delay took us away from the revision and the tribe for almost two years. At our annual field conference, the dorm parents talked with us about problems Melanie was having with her stomach and perhaps her gallbladder. In one of the meetings, the school nurse sat behind her. She asked to talk with us after the meeting. Based on her examination, she said that Melanie had a curvature of the spine and it was pushing her organs to one side, and this could be the possible reason for the problems she was having. The doctor recommended that we take her back to the States to have it checked out and start whatever treatment was necessary without delay.

This was another experience where we could look back and see how God went before us and prepared the way. We had no idea where to start and little finances to face what was ahead. The pastor of our home church knew a well-known retired missionary orthopedic surgeon in Greenville, South Carolina. Our pastor went with us to see him. After he examined Melanie, he confirmed what the nurse in TamaTama diagnosed. More examinations showed that she had a 45-degree curvature of the spine and without surgery, it would continue to get worse and damage her organs. He also had contacts with the Shriners Hospital in Greenville and made it possible for the surgery to be done free of cost.

Translation

We were on a waiting list until space became available. In January of the following year they contacted us with news that they had an opening for her. The surgery was performed, and an 8" permanent stainless-steel rod was inserted in her spine. This was a very hard surgery for her, but it was completely successful. After many months of wearing a cast and more follow-up check-ups, she was released to return to Venezuela with us.

We returned to Venezuela and back to the revision of the New Testament. When the revision was finished, it was re-checked by two of NTM's most knowledgeable translation checkers which upon their checking required another complete typing. Finally, it was finished and sent off to the Venezuelan Bible Society in Caracas, where they started making the printing plates. They wanted us to check it once again after they typed it, which was a good thing. When we received their copy back, we were shocked to find large numbers of pages that were typed incorrectly. It looked like someone had their fingers on the wrong keys and kept typing without looking at it. So those pages had to be redone. The New Testament manuscripts

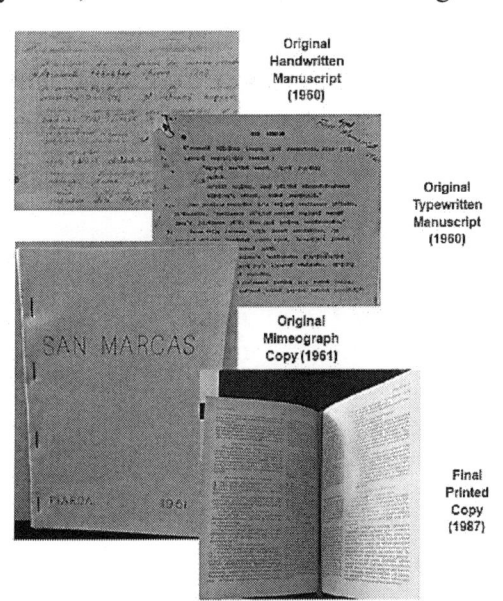

Original Handwritten Manuscript (1960)

Original Typewritten Manuscript (1960)

Original Mimeograph Copy (1961)

Final Printed Copy (1987)

Journey into the Unknown

were checked again, and more changes made with the help of our co-workers in both typing and proofreading. While we waited for the printing of the New Testament to be finished, it was suggested by the Bible Society that we contact the Venezuelan churches in the country and present to them the Piaroa New Testament project as well as the finances necessary for printing. This was a learning experience for us and unbeknown to us, it was preparation for a future ministry.

In Their Hands

The day had finally arrived. Sunday, February 1, 1987, the Piaroa tribe received their New Testament in one volume. After more than a twenty-seven-year struggle with all manner of delays, interruptions, and difficulties, Satan had lost the battle! After all these years of seeing the manuscripts pass from translators' hands to the typists' hands to the translator helpers' hands to checkers' hands and finally to the printers, it was now in **their** hands...in the hands of the Piaroas for whom the project was undertaken decades before.

Arrival of New Testament via Plane

On January 30, the first part of a two-day presentation program took place in the City Hall of Puerto Ayacucho. The Venezuelan Bible Society officially turned over the New Testaments in the Piaroa language to New Tribes

Translation

Mission. On hand for the celebration were government officials, evangelical lea ders, and friends of NTM from all over Venezuela. Each government representative received a complimentary copy of the Piaroa New Testament. Reverend Asdrubal Rios, a well-known evangelical leader, publisher, and politician, delivered a message focusing on the importance of the Word. Then all the pastors present filed to the platform for prayer as the Piaroa New Testament was formally dedicated to the honor of the Lord and the blessing of the Piaroa Church.

Dedication of Piaroa New Testament

The following day, about seventy visitors were transported to the Piaroa village of Pendare for the presentation of the New Testament to the tribe. There were around seven hundred Piaroas who attended from various villages far and near. The village church that had seemed so big only held half the people. Many had to stay outside, but those who were fortunate enough to be near the screenless windows could lean through the windows into the building and watch the proceedings. It was a three-hour service in which many outside speakers addressed the crowd through an

Overflow of Piaroas for Ceremony

Journey into the Unknown

interpreter, a choir of Piaroa children gave a musical program in both Spanish and Piaroa, and finally, the New Testament was presented.

Each of the missionaries and the language helpers, who had worked on the translation project down through the years, was presented with a copy of the New Testament. Then all Piaroa church leaders were given copies of the long-awaited book. They were at the front of church when they received their New Testaments, and, once they had them in their hands, they turned to face the congregation with smiles on their faces. It was with uncontrollable tears of great joy that we watched them raise their hands with their New Testaments! Praise the Lord! The day had finally come, and the Piaroa New Testament was in their hands!

Journey into the Unknown

Chapter 18 - A Change of Ministry

"Behold I set before you an open door...."
Revelation 3:8a.

This verse came to mind many times during our journey serving the Lord in Venezuela. We continually asked the Lord to either "open the door" to what He wanted us to do or to "shut the door" if it was not His will.

We desperately wanted Venezuelan believers to become involved in reaching their own people, especially the unreached indigenous people living in the jungles. However, we were very much involved in translation, church planting, and teaching in the Piaroa tribe. We saw how the Lord started sending more laborers to work with the Piaroas.

Looking back, we can see how the Lord was preparing us for this next step. Even though we were still living and working with the Piaroas, we made trips to different cities for missionary conferences and raised money for printing the New Testament. This opened many doors for contacting pastors and churches all over the country.

One day, while still in San Juan, we were surprised when we heard the distant sounds of planes coming close to the village. When we went outside to look, we saw two small planes flying in front of our house. We knew that it was not our mission plane, so we assumed it was visitors to the Catholic mission which was located a short distance upriver from us. After a while, we heard a knock on our door, and there were two American couples and two small children.

A Change of Ministry

They heard about the tribes in the southern part of Venezuela and wanted to visit them. They came in two different planes. When they heard that there were Americans there, they wanted to meet us and see what help we could be to them in their adventure. They wanted to stay with us also (we always looked forward to having someone to talk with from our homeland). Since our children were away at school, we had two empty bedrooms. One family had to return to Caracas the next day, but the other family with two young children stayed with us a couple days.

We explained who we were and why we were there, and we quickly became friends. We visited some villages with them, so they could get an idea of lifestyle with the people. In one of these villages, they were celebrating a typical Piaroa festival. When they left, they were so impressed that they started talking with others about it at the U.S. Embassy gatherings in Caracas.

As a result, Fred was invited to speak at one of their meetings in the home of the Vice Ambassador. Over 100 Americans attended, both embassy personnel and business people working in Caracas. They wanted Fred to speak about what it was like for a North American boy to be raised in the jungles…I wondered if they were looking for another Tarzan! They told Fred to speak about his experiences but not to preach! We were surprised to find that there were several pastors and their wives in the group. There "just happened" to be a conference of some church groups in Caracas at that time and some of them wanted to come and hear about the tribal people.

Fred spoke and showed a slide presentation the first 35 minutes, and then opened it up for questions. One of the questions was, "Why do you think you need to take your Christian faith to these people? Why don't you leave them alone?" Fred looked to the lady in charge who had requested that he not preach, and said, "Carol, I am going to have to preach." She said, "go ahead," and he did. He gave the plan of salvation so clearly that a child could understand. He also took the opportunity to talk about the "Great Commission" and how we as Christians are responsible (commanded - Mark 16:15) to take the Gospel to them. When he told them that many tribal people had asked, "Why has no one come sooner to tell us about the Gospel? Our parents and grandparents have died without hearing the Gospel." There was stunned silence.

The Lord allowed Fred to witness to these people through the questions they asked. Many people came up to us afterwards and commented on how well Fred answered the questions, that he gave honest answers and did not try to dodge the issue. We felt this was a divinely ordained opportunity that the Lord brought about, and it was a joy to be a part of it.

In the 1980's, a new branch of NTM work was started called "Representation Work." This meant that the missionaries would represent NTM in the Spanish-speaking churches in the country. They would promote tribal mission work to people in the churches along with challenging them to become involved in evangelizing indigenous groups in their own country. Also, the Venezuelan Bible Society requested that a member of NTM go with them to promote the New Testament printing project. They needed more funding to finish, and they really wanted the Venezuelans Christians to be an integral part of the project.

A Change of Ministry

Wilford Neese was one of the first NTM missionaries to do this. He traveled to different churches promoting the funding needed for printing the Yanomamo (Guaica) New Testament translation. There were others that worked on this in different areas of the country. We became a part of this team in 1985, after the unexpected death of Wally Jank who was representing NTM on the eastern side of Venezuela. His widow, Marg Jank, requested that we move to Ciudad Bolivar to be close to where she was teaching Spanish to the new missionaries. It seemed like a good place for us to start as we could at the same time be close enough to help Marg when needed. We moved to Puerto Ordaz, a short drive from Ciudad Bolivar. Puerto Ordaz had a population of about one million people and was one of the most industrialized cities of Venezuela. There were more evangelical churches and greater possibilities for outreach.

We made weekly trips to Ciudad Bolivar to help Marg with the Spanish course and other needs. One of our responsibilities was to find housing for new missionaries, a challenging proposition when factoring in the paperwork, security concerns, and budget limitations.

We went to this area with the idea that gaining entrance into these churches would take a long time. We thought we would have to work hard to win their trust due to many false accusations against NTM by those who wanted us out of the country. However, we found it to be just the opposite. We were amazed at how many pastors reached out to us and asked if we would come to their church to speak. We had so many requests we had to turn some down.

Journey into the Unknown

During this time, there was an established Missionary Training Institute, for Spanish speaking people, in the neighboring country of Colombia which trained future missionaries from both Colombia and Venezuela. A national couple and single girl had already finished training at the Institute. They became the first Venezuelan Missionaries the same year we joined the representation team. The number of students were growing.

When the Venezuelan students at the Colombia NTM training institute came back to Venezuela on school vacations, we were privileged to have some of them travel with us. This was a real boost to the Venezuelan church meetings for promoting missions. These students shared

Student Ministry

their testimonies of how the Lord led them to prepare for missionary training. It was one thing for us, foreigners, to challenge others in a foreign country to be missionaries, but quite another thing for one of their own to challenge them. It made quite an impact.

At one seminar on missions, a Brazilian born pastor, who had come to Venezuela to plant a church, was in attendance. He was challenged to get his church involved in tribal missions. He asked Fred to speak in his church. After he spoke, the pastor asked if we had a missionary that their church could help support. We did have one, the very first

A Change of Ministry

Venezuelan missionary who had finished their NTM training in Colombia. So, this missionary and his wife accompanied us to the church and gave their testimonies. As the Lord led them, the church started supporting the missionaries. This was a real joy for us to see God's desires, and ours, fulfilled. We had already been challenging the Venezuelan people to be missionaries themselves, and now we were also actively challenging the local pastors and churches to support these missionaries with prayers and finances.

Ramon and Omaira Mendoza

Another blessing to our team was to have a retired Venezuelan military man and his wife, Ramon and Omaira Mendoza, join us. They were such an important part of our being accepted in the churches. Ramon, of course, could relate better to his own people than we could. One thing he did, which was difficult for others on the team, was make frequent trips to Colombia to visit the students at the training institute and encourage them. Ramon also took care of receiving and sending the students' financial aid from their supporters. To do this he would have to make trips to the Colombian border every month to deposit their financial aid in a Colombian bank. Ramon also taught us more about the Venezuelan culture, what to do and what not to do in certain circumstances, and to better understand the laws of Venezuela.

Journey into the Unknown

On one of the students' school vacations, they shared with us some of their fears. They said it was going to be hard to go back, as there was a lot of guerrilla activity in the country. Before she left for vacation, a letter had been sent to every house saying the guerrillas were going to take over the town where the school was located. The hospitals and clinics were advised to be ready in case there was bloodshed. The missionary staff had met to make plans for an escape should this happen. Fred was planning on making a trip over there, but many advised him against it. This news confirmed that he shouldn't go.

The guerrilla threat along with the danger of young people traveling back and forth across the border brought fear to the parents and the churches of Venezuela. They were also concerned about the cost to send their young people to another country to study. They would often ask us, "Why doesn't NTM start their own training school here in Venezuela?" All we could say to them was to pray that if it was God's will, He would bring it about.

Due to traveling from one side of Venezuela to the other and as far south as the road would go, car trouble became a part of life. Venezuela had 700 miles of road from east to west and 500 from north to south. We made this trip many times and what started out as one repair on one trip turned into three repairs on the next. There were times when we had the missionary students traveling with us, so the condition of our vehicle was a concern to us.

On one occasion, we pulled off the side of the road because the car sounded like it was going to fall apart. Shortly after we stopped, a small truck that was overheated pulled up in front of us. Fred went to talk to them and was looking

A Change of Ministry

under the hood of their truck to see if he could help. I was sitting in our car when I saw fire coming out from the back of their truck and they could not see it. I quickly got out telling them that their truck was on fire. We had a fire extinguisher in our car, so Fred put the fire out. Fortunately, they fixed their truck. Then, they offered to look at our car. They found that our problem was a fuel pump, and we had an extra one with us just in case. (Yep, that's right; we carried around extra fuel pumps!!!) They were able to fix our car, so we could go on to our destination. Fred told the mechanic we were sorry about his truck overheating and catching on fire but explained that God had sent them for us.

On another occasion, we were on our way to Puerto Ayacucho, a twelve-hour trip from Puerto Ordaz. Most of this trip was on a very deserted dirt road at that time. We had car trouble again and Fred tried everything he knew to fix it with no success. We sat in the car for five hours. As we had a lot of time to talk, this verse came to our minds. *"In everything give thanks: for this is the will of God in Christ Jesus concerning you." 1 Thess. 5:18.* So many times since the beginning of our journey we remembered that verse and experienced the reality of it. We thought of the many things we could be thankful for instead of fretting over our situation. We were encouraged as we remembered how God always worked everything out. The heat of the day was so bad that we decided to try and push the car to a shade tree not too far off. As we were doing this, a car came by and stopped to ask us what our problem was. The same thing happened as in the previous occasion. One of the men was a mechanic, and he told us it was the fuel pump. He fixed it enough for us to get to Puerto Ayacucho

Journey into the Unknown

where we had it fixed and bought another fuel pump to keep in the car just in case. Spare fuel pumps proved to be a good idea as they were needed when the car broke down yet again in downtown Caracas, the largest city in Venezuela.

Car Being Towed

Mechanics stopping to help did not happen on some other trips, however, like when we had to get a tow truck to tow us for two and a half hours to our mission home outside of Caracas. The difference this time was that the wrecker came with another passenger, so they told us to sit in our car. That was a surprise! We sat in our car with the front end jacked up while we were towed through the heart of Caracas! When we reflected upon these incidents, we saw how God protected us...and had a sense of humor!

When we felt we could no longer continue a traveling ministry with all the car trouble that was draining all our support, we started praying about what we should do. Did the Lord have something different for us that would mean less traveling? We wrote a letter to our supporting churches and individuals and asked them to pray concerning this matter. We cut back on long distance traveling and only had services in churches close by. At the same time one of the members of our team left for the U.S. on home assignment and left the western side of Venezuela uncovered.

A Change of Ministry

One day we received a letter from a supporting church telling us that a member had passed away and left an inheritance. The church leaders decided to use some

New Bronco

of it to help us buy a new car. They wanted us to get a good, sturdy car or a four-wheel drive that would meet the needs of our ministry with room for taking missionary students with us. In addition, another supporter sent us enough money to finish what we lacked in buying a four-wheel-drive Ford Bronco plus added expenses that came with buying a car. We were so thankful for this answer to prayer. We took that to mean the Lord wanted us to continue doing the same as before...visiting different areas and challenging people.

The Bronco was assembled in a city about an hour from us. When we put in an order for it, we chose a less expensive model. When it was finished, we went to the dealers to pick it up, but we had quite a surprise awaiting us. Fred tried to tell the man that the car he was showing us was not the car we ordered. He said, "this was the one they told me was for you." The car they said was ours was the "top of the line" with all the extras. We thought for sure they were mistaken and were afraid to accept the car without confirmation that it was really our car. We later found out the man that sent it to us from the factory was a Christian and wanted us to have the best at the same price as the cheaper one. We felt God had given us a Cadillac! So many times, we limit God

Journey into the Unknown

when asking things from Him. He gives us so much more than what we ask or think.

The Bronco was used for many different things. One trip was to the Venezuelan/Colombian border to take two students as far as we could to the Institute in Colombia. We could not cross the border without visas, but they would be able to go the rest of the way by bus. However, they did not have enough money to buy a bus ticket, so we paid for the tickets. We figured that we had enough money left to get us home.

As we were driving through the Andes mountains on our way home, Fred began to get sleepy. I turned the car radio on to keep him awake, and for the first time, we learned that civil unrest had broken out in Venezuela. There was an attempt to oust Carlos Andres Perez, the new president. The president was talking to the public and warned everyone of a coup attempt and that there would be a "toque de queda", a curfew, country wide and anyone that was out on the street after 5 p.m. would be in danger. It was about 4 p.m. when we heard this. We were getting close to one of the larger cities in the country and could find a hotel in which to stay. The hotel we found was very expensive, but they did have an off-street parking lot which would help keep our car safe. Since this was an unexpected expense, we asked them if they would accept a credit card from the U.S. When we were settled in, we made a call to our Venezuelan co-worker, Ramon Mendoza, the retired military man. He advised us to stay in the hotel and not go outside or try to leave until he called and let us know if it would be safe. This would have been the envy of anyone to stay in one of the nicest hotels in the country, but it was

A Change of Ministry

clouded with wondering what was happening in the country and thinking of how much this would cost. The first night was the scariest as we could hear shooting and rioting out in the street. We took a fast peek out the window, and it didn't look good as we could see tanks going up and down the street. I must admit, I had nightmares that night. However, as we prayed we committed our lives and the lives of the Venezuelan people to the Lord. He gave us peace.

This continued for three days. The next time we called Ramon, he told us it would be safe to travel. He said since it would take two days to arrive home, we should stop somewhere early before curfew time. Since we didn't know the town where we stopped, we had to choose the only hotel available. We later found out that it was an X-rated hotel, but once again God's presence and protection was over us.

The next morning before leaving the "hotel," we called Ramon again to see if it was safe for us to continue. He told us that we could, but that we shouldn't go the main route that we usually took. He said we should take a short-cut that was mainly dirt roads with many pot-holes as the main road was blocked with demonstrations which we could get caught in. We had used this short-cut before on previous trips, and it was not the most desirable route. Under the circumstances, however, this seemed to be our best option. There would be very few homes or places to get help, if we needed it. It was a hard decision to make, but we thought the Lord wanted us to take the dark, lonely, back road. It was dark by the time we reached it, and we were going along at a good pace when we hit a bad pot-hole which caused a blow-out. When Fred got out to look at the damage, he discovered that the road was completely washed out a hundred feet ahead. Thank God for the blow-out!! It was another reminder that at times we go through difficult situations that we can't understand, but

> *"...God works ALL things out for our good." Romans 8:28.*

During the weeks when we did not travel, we helped teach orientation and culture classes to the new NTM arrivals. We had a scare when one of the new missionaries hit a drunken man walking across the road in front of him. It wasn't the new missionary's fault, but in Venezuela if you hit someone, you were supposed to go to jail. Then two other students had wrecks. The biggest scare, though, was when one of the students was asked to take a suitcase from one place to another. He wanted to be a friend and helpful, so he took it. We later found that there was something questionable in it, which could have led to serious trouble for him. These students could have ended up with jail time, but we once again saw God's love and intervention. These were all good examples of why it was important to know the culture and ways of the people.

We enjoyed getting to know the new missionaries when they arrived, and we often invited them to our house to spend the weekend. This gave them a break from language study and gave us time to get to know them and help them as they started on their journey.

We also opened our home up to prospective Venezuelan missionary students. We helped prepare them for what to expect at the Missionary Training Institute. We emphasized

A Change of Ministry

that "the World is the harvest field" and to seek God's will where He would have them go. When they finished their training, we went over the operations of NTM in their country and answered their questions. This proved to strengthen the bond between the two cultures.

We were in this new ministry over four years and were making plans for our home assignment. We reconsidered our location and how we could be more centrally located in the country. We decided that when we returned from the U.S., we would move to Maracay, another one of the larger cities known as "the crossroads of Venezuela." This would shorten our driving time. We packed our belongings and stored them while we were away. Another blessing came our way when two Christian doctors, a husband and wife, were transferred to Puerto Ordaz. They were looking for a home to rent, and we were both blessed by them taking over our house. They also let us store our belongings in an extra room they didn't need while we were out of the country.

During this time of packing, Fred was still scheduled to speak at several mission conferences. He was also committed to helping other groups of new missionary candidates get to Colombia to start their training. We received an unexpected call from our daughter Melanie, who stayed back in the States after finishing college. My dad was in the hospital, seriously ill, and the doctor did not expect him to live through the night. I went home to be with Mom as Fred stayed behind to finish packing and to complete the meetings that were already scheduled.

After arriving back home, we saw how God led us to go home early. Dad had improved even though the doctors could not understand why he was still alive. It was evident that Mom really needed help as she was so tired but never asked us to come home. The day after I arrived, my brother, David, and his family arrived from Panama. The Lord allowed us to be with Dad the day He took him home several months later. We were thankful that we were there with Norman, my second oldest brother, as he was alone in taking care of our parents. We were there together and helped Mom during this time.

Another reason we felt we should be home was for Melanie and Brian. Melanie continued working at the Clearwater Christian College office after graduation. She studied to be an executive secretary and was in the process of switching jobs. She and Brian shared an apartment as he continued studying at ITT. He was in his final year and would graduate soon. Brian went as far as he could in studying electronic engineering in Tampa, Florida. His professors encouraged him to further his study in Indianapolis, Indiana, where he could get his bachelor's degree in electronic engineering.

The Lord used a family that we knew for years, Jim and Janet Keim, to meet our needs. We were members of the same church when Brian was a baby. We lost contact with them through the years but our co-worker, Gene Miller, was Jim's cousin. We contacted Gene and he gave us the Keim's phone number. When they heard that Brian would be moving to Indianapolis, they offered to help him find a place to live and to take him to the church where they were members. This was a blessing and relief to us.

The rest of our time we contacted our supporters, went to medical check-ups, and spent time with our family who were now in four different locations. Brian did very well in Indianapolis. He found a very special girl, who happened to be the Keim's youngest daughter, Jody. This was not the first time that he saw Jody, although neither remembers. In 1969, they were together in the Westerville Bible Church nursery where both families were members. In February, before we returned to Venezuela, they announced their engagement and set a date for the wedding. We knew that we would be making another trip back in the fall.

It was never easy to say good-bye but knowing both children were settled in their jobs and in homes made it easier. The hardest part was saying good-bye to my mom. She was alone in a large three-story house, but she did not want to keep us from going back to Venezuela. While saying our goodbyes to her, we told her that we would see her next year when we came back for her grandson's wedding. We returned to Venezuela on January 24, 1991.

Mom was not a person to remain idle. After 22 years of taking care of her quadriplegic husband, she flourished and was always finding a way to serve the Lord. She started a new project making cassette tapes with a message on prophecy and God's plan of salvation. She sent them to the troops in active service in the Gulf war, Desert Storm. A local television station came to her house to interview her and take pictures of her as she had already sent out 6,000 tapes. Two weeks from the day we returned to Venezuela and while in Maracay "house hunting," we received a call from our daughter. She gave us the news that Mom had passed away that day. She was alone and in bed like she was taking a nap. She peacefully went to be with the Lord.

Journey into the Unknown

It had been almost eight months from the day that our Dad went to be with the Lord.

This is what her three children wrote about her:

> *"Her children rise up and call her blessed;"*
> *Proverbs 31:28a.*

For those who knew Mom, and especially her children, we have no better way of expressing our feelings other than by this verse. We feel blessed to have been her children and to have had the example of Mom and Dad's lives to guide us through the years. Mom's work on earth ended February 7, 1991, when she peacefully went into the presence of the Lord, whom she loved and served to the very end.

Journey into the Unknown

Chapter 19 – Missionary Training Institute

"Study to show thyself approved unto God, a workman that need not to be ashamed, rightly dividing the word of truth." 2 Timothy 2:15.

We were very thankful that New Tribes Mission had made provision for training from their beginning days. NTM put much emphasis on thorough preparation and had training centers in the States and in other countries. However, since we had no training center in Venezuela, we sent our new students to the missionary training center in the neighboring country of Colombia.

Unfortunately, it was a difficult situation in Colombia due to an increase in guerrilla activity. The Colombian training institute moved their classes from Fusagasugá to a smaller location in Bogota, because the guerrillas took over the town. They asked us not to send any more students to them as they were trying to get the current ones through the training. Under these circumstances, they could not accept any more. They thought it might be a couple years before they could accept more. However, the interest amongst the young people was greater than ever. We needed a Venezuelan training institute.

On the western side of Venezuela, in the foot-hills of the Andes Mountains, a pastor told us about some property that might be available. The property belonged to Team Mission and an orphanage was built on it in the early days. Years later, it was used by the Venezuelan branch of Team Mission for the care of elderly homeless people. The pastor

Missionary Training Institute

accompanied us to visit the property in the small picturesque town of Betijoque. This was an agricultural town of 12,000 people, and farming was their main source of income. In the past, Fred and students from the Colombia Institute visited many small churches located in the surrounding area. While speaking at these churches, they had slept in the Team Mission orphanage building. They had arrived late at night, and they left early the next morning before they could look around the property.

Aerial View of CFM Property

This time we visited the old orphanage property during the daylight with the idea of using it as an institute instead of just a place to sleep. We were amazed at the size and potential of this property. It was much larger than we expected. We were very cognizant of the run-down condition of the building and property as it had been all but abandoned for some time. Still, we could envision beginning the first two-year phase of the Institute there. There was enough land to complete the construction of the buildings needed for the training program, all three phases, as well as staff housing.

This location was an answer to prayer for us. Before seriously looking for a location for the Institute, we had previously felt it would be good to locate in a lower cost-of-living area, not near a large city. Also, we wanted it to

Journey into the Unknown

be in an area where there would be small towns close by for the students to have a ministry while in training. Lastly, we felt it was important to not locate too close to the border, due to the rise in guerrilla activity. This location satisfied all those needs.

We contacted the owners of the property and told them of our desire for NTM to buy a place for a missionary training Institute. The owners said they did not know what to do with the property as it was very run down. They didn't have the money to repair it or any plans to use it. They expressed their concern that the property would be taken away from them due to the run-down condition. They were very interested in what we were proposing and the vice-president of Ovice, the Spanish branch of Team Mission, made the comment, "This is like a gift from God that NTM would be interested in the property." We agreed!

Signing CFM Documents

The owners requested a letter explaining how we wanted to use the property. After months of talks, prayers, phone calls, paper work, and many miles of traveling from our home to the location, Fred signed a five-year lease with an option to buy. Team Mission leaders decided that the lease payment would be covered by the cost of repairs and building what was needed for the institute. We had hoped to buy property instead of leasing, but this would give us five more years to keep looking and seeking God's leading

Missionary Training Institute

for a permanent place. With the signing of this agreement, we could start classes the next year. It took our leaders by surprise when we told them we had found a place! After ten years of praying, the Lord answered our prayers.

During the seven-hour drive to visit the property after leasing it, we were so excited. At the same time, the unknown and the job ahead of us was overwhelming. We parked in front of the gate and could hardly see the big two-story building (with an unfinished second floor) much less the rest of the 15 acres of overgrown land which reminded us of the jungles. However, we knew that this was God's answer to many prayers, and this was the place for a missionary training institute. We were reminded of what David said to his son Solomon,

"Be strong and of good courage, and do it; do not fear nor be dismayed, for the Lord God - my God - will be with you. He will not leave you nor forsake you, until you have finished all the work for the service of the house of the Lord." 1 Chronicles 28:20

Fred In Makeshift Kitchen

As we unloaded the Bronco, we found out that there had not been any water for the past week and a half. How would we clean without water? How would we cook? How would we do many things? The electricity was just about as bad as the plumbing. There were only a few light bulbs working in the building and much of the wiring was stolen or in poor condition. The bathrooms were without water. Fortunately,

Journey into the Unknown

Fred found a small stream of water by the road, so we carried in water by buckets from this stream for cleaning.

It was finally time to set up a temporary kitchen in the apartment for us and the Garcias. They were a Venezuelan couple who had finished the Colombian institute and agreed to come to this school and oversee the remodeling. The camping equipment we unloaded would be the kitchen appliances. They would be there in a month, so we hurriedly prepared for them.

Barbara In Makeshift Kitchen

As the day passed, we wondered where we were going to sleep as this building was without furniture of any kind. Since we knew no one in the area, we drove around to see if there was a hotel in Betijoque. Finally, we found the one and only hotel. By most standards, it would be rated as a minus four stars. The hotel had a bed, a shower over the toilet, and a sink beside the bed, and a small air conditioner that was almost on the floor. That was all we needed and after a full day of working with what we had available, it felt like a five-star hotel when we laid our heads down to sleep.

The next day, Fred's first job was to dig up old broken pipes and replace them to get water to the building. This was not an easy task as he was alone. He dug as far as he could until he got to the road. He knew that he had to get permission from the local authorities to dig up the old pipes that ran under the road. This would involve breaking up the

Missionary Training Institute

road and causing a traffic problem. He was so thankful for the little stream of water we had until all this work was completed.

Fred Putting in Water Pipes

Two weeks later, we returned to our home in Maracay for meetings. During this time, Fred made a kitchen cabinet in our back yard for the Betijoque apartment. We found ourselves dreaming about all the things needed to get started there. He made cabinets in his sleep, as I made curtains for the windows in my sleep. It was an exciting time!

Once we returned, we found out a church in Barquisimeto, a medium-sized city three to four hours from Betijoque, was interested in helping to prepare the Institute. Among the young people in the church was a young fellow, Marcos Brito, whom Fred had met in other churches where he presented mission needs. Fred noticed that Marcos seemed to be present in different churches where he was speaking. Marcos expressed his interest in missions. This church sent the first group to help with the Institute building repairs. Marcos, his

First Work Group

Journey into the Unknown

fiancé Eliana, his mother, and several others from the church made up the first work team. Volunteers and contributions came from all over Venezuela and the U.S. for construction materials throughout the project.

The remodeling of the Institute progressed, and we finally needed teachers and staff. The Lord met that need. He even provided a director as a missionary family from the Colombian Institute staff transferred to Venezuela. When we heard they were coming to Venezuela, we prayed that they would be willing to come as director of the Institute. This was another answer to prayer when they accepted this position. They had a real heart for the Venezuelans and the Institute and were very happy to be a part of this ministry. This was a blessing to us as we had the vision to train future missionaries but had no experience in it. The Lord put together the team that He knew was needed. There were enough staff members to start the Institute, and we returned to our full-time ministry in Maracay: challenging young people and churches to become involved in tribal missions. We promised to return and participate in a missionary conference, and the timing was perfect.

While in Maracay, we still made short trips back to Betijoque to help. However, after less than a year, we were asked to pray about moving to Betijoque to be part of the staff. Fred would be the administrator and coordinator in charge of student ministries with the churches. On the weekends, we could visit churches as mission representatives challenging Venezuelans to tribal missions.

The decision we had to make concerning another move was a heart wrenching one for us. We prayed for so many years and challenged others to pray for an institute. Were we

Missionary Training Institute

willing to give up our current ministry for the institute ministry? Were we supposed to somehow do both? Could we trust the Lord to work out the distance and time issue with filling both ministries at the same time? If we moved here, how could we get out of the contract that we signed for the house we were renting? As these thoughts came to mind, we were finally reminded that if this was God's will for us, He would give us wisdom and peace in what we should do. We started praying about these questions, and the Lord gave us peace. We set a date to move from the "Crossroads of Venezuela," Maracay, to Betijoque, a seven-hour drive away. We saw the Lord work out all the details, and we trusted He would resolve all our concerns. Three months later we moved to Betijoque where we found a small house to rent.

As the word spread about the beginning of a missionary training Institute and all that was involved in getting it ready for the first class, we started receiving letters from individuals and church groups in both the U.S. and Venezuela. They wanted to volunteer to help with this project. Some brought money to pay for the materials needed. Others sent monetary gifts to go towards the construction. We were so blessed as we saw the Lord do what seemed impossible. There were still many jobs to be done before classes started. One group painted. Another installed a water tank and repaired the water system. During this time, we received a call from the owners of the property. They were ready to sell it to the mission. This was a relief as we no longer had to find another place and could continue with the construction needed for the three phases of the training program. Another confirmation that this was God's plan in action, and that He would provide!

Journey into the Unknown

The big day arrived on August 24, 1997. We inaugurated the CFM (initials for Missionary Training Center/Center for Forming Missionaries, in Spanish). There were 60 people or so in attendance at the celebration. The program consisted of welcoming the visitors, explaining the purpose and goals of CFM, and the plans for construction. The staff was comprised of both Venezuelans and North Americans. It was an added blessing to have five local pastors with us. The first class started with seven students, who were introduced during the service. In this class were two Brazilians, one Colombian and four Venezuelans.

After the inauguration, someone came up to me and asked, "How does it feel to have finally arrived to this point"? I compared it to the same feeling that we had on the day of the Piaroa New Testament presentation. It represents a day of victory after many years of hard work, struggles, and lots of delays, sweat and tears. Most of all, it represented years of prayers by God's children from home and abroad. All of them resoundingly answered!

As the Institute construction progressed, two more church groups came down to work on the buildings of the next phase of the training. This was not only a great provision from the Lord but also an example to the students who had left their families

Second Work Group

and jobs to give of themselves to prepare for tribal missions. There seemed to be a continual change of

Missionary Training Institute

personnel, but the Lord always supplied replacements. The Lord had provided money to build the administrator's house on the property which enabled us to move. The timing was perfect as the owner of our rented house wanted it back; that was the pattern with us and house renting. We marveled as God met our every need even before we knew there would be one.

When the director moved to minister in a tribe, we were asked to fill in his position until there was a replacement. This involved being the coordinator of all three stages of the training as the work progressed. During this time, a group from two different states, Iowa and Maine, came down to build apartments for the missionary course staff. This was the third time that people from these states had joined together to help us. This was probably their hardest visit. The first two days they worked hard and fast, and we were amazed at how quickly the walls were going up. However, this came to a fast stop when all but two of them became very sick with a virus.

At the same time, we received a written letter from the local government telling us that all construction had to stop. Their reasoning was that we did not have permission to build on the property. The group of people helping continued to do other things that were not considered construction, like painting the main building and cleaning brush from the property. Although their construction goal was not accomplished, their attitude of acceptance, that there was a purpose in all of this, and their belief that God was in control was a great example to the students. More groups were making plans to come down, but their visits

Journey into the Unknown

were postponed until the problem with the building permits was resolved.

Fourteen months later the town council granted us the permit after they received a letter from our lawyer. In that letter, he stated that if they didn't settle the problem by a certain date he would take it to a higher court. This letter resulted in a visit from seven council members to talk about our "destiny"...that was the word they used in their letter to us. The Lord used this visit to help us. The council members walked around the property, and as they did that, they saw what CFM was doing and what our purpose was. When they left, they were all in favor of settling the problem immediately. They assured us that the decision would be fully favorable to us. Some wanted to give us permission to build on the spot, but this wasn't possible as there was still some legal work involved such as surveying the land and charging us for taxes due. We finally received permission in writing to finish all the construction projects that were planned for all the property after the taxes were paid. There were nine more buildings to be built, one of which was a dormitory for the Spanish-speaking missionary children.

We sent word out to church groups that they could resume coming to Betijoque to volunteer for construction work at the institute. We were responsible for these groups as most of the CFM staff did not speak English. Often in the evenings, after a long day of work, these helpers would gather on our front porch for a time of fellowship and prayer. What a sweet time that was as we reflected on what God did and would continue to do. Words were not enough to explain how all of us were blessed by these church

Missionary Training Institute

groups. They not only worked hard and provided support, but their examples encouraged both the staff and the students.

We regularly saw God work all things out in His time and way. We were encouraged anew every day to challenge and prepare Venezuelans for evangelism both at home and in all the world.

Before   **After**

"And he said unto them, Go ye into all the world, and preach the gospel to every creature." Mark 16:15

Chapter 20 – CFM in Action

We continued our institute ministry with the students. One of the ministry outreaches included a trip to the grasslands of Venezuela. These took place during Easter break. It was a time when most businesses closed, and people headed for the beach, the mountains or just anywhere to get away from home and have a relaxing time. The evangelical churches often used that week for Bible retreats and outreaches to areas with little or no Biblical teaching. Fred, with another professor and several students decided to make an evangelistic trip to the grasslands.

After leaving the road and driving miles over tractor and cow trails, the men found a large group of hungry souls ready to be taught God's Word. We, and most missionaries, thought that tribal people were the neediest and most neglected. However, after spending a week in the grasslands, Fred realized these people were just as needy. They were farmers and ranchers and it became apparent that they were very isolated from the outside world. The only difference between the tribal and grassland people was that the grassland people spoke Spanish and had some small contact with civilization.

There were a few churches scattered over a one-hundred-mile area. Nationals from local churches started these little church plants but left after very little teaching. It turned out the nationals chose a person from the grassland group that was more responsible and designated them as the pastor of that church. At one church, the pastor could not read, so a child read the scripture to him. Then the pastor preached on that verse. There was such a need for teaching amongst these churches.

It moved us to watch people come on donkeys, by foot, and even by oxen. One mother walked several hours each way with a baby in her arms and small children at her side. Some made this trip in the morning, spent the day listening to teaching, and then returned home at 10:30 at night after the evening service ended. They repeated the same trip the next morning. Over the seven days the group was there, they held 13 meetings. As Fred and the teachers and students left, the people begged them to come back.

The last trip to the grasslands that Fred and his group made while we were still at the Institute was Easter week vacation of 2000. Little did they know what was in store for them this time. After they arrived at their first stop at the edge of the grasslands, the pastor (the coordinator for the area) gave them their itinerary. They were to have meetings in 11 churches during that week. They would end with a final meeting on Easter Sunday night. Fred, the teachers, and the students from the Institute left town around 1:00 p.m. on a Sunday and began their trip. After two hours of seeing very little except grasslands and woods, they arrived at a little settlement of four houses where they picked up a guide. As they continued, a student traveling with them asked if there were any people living in these woods. They told him to wait and see. That night around 150 people were in the first service. They came from as far as two hours away. Even the unbelievers came to all these meetings, because there literally was nothing else to do.

The next day, Monday, they left that church and went to two more churches. As they traveled, their diet initially

Journey into the Unknown

consisted of plain spaghetti cooked with cooking oil or rice and goat meat. This was served three times a day. Bathroom facilities were the open woods for everyone including those that lived there. Shower facilities were a five-gallon bucket of water with a gourd for a dipper behind a partial wall. Sleeping facilities were a hammock hung out in the open woods under the starry sky.

During this trip, the Venezuelan professor, Gilberto, was asked to perform his first marriage. People began arriving at 3:00 p.m. for the 8:00 p.m. wedding. Four hundred people were there that night and all of them had to be fed. They killed a cow for the occasion and nothing was wasted. Donkeys, mules, and 100 bicycles were lined up and tied to the fence for 200 feet. Since people came from so far away, they had a service after the wedding which went until 4:00 a.m. What an experience!

The next day, they moved on to keep to their schedule. In all, they had 16 meetings in 12 different churches in ten days...and a wedding!! They returned the day before classes started again at the institute with a renewed vision.

Over the years, we experienced good times and hard times at CFM. Once we bought the property, God blessed the institute even though Satan did his best to fight us. God used these bad times to teach us, as well as the students, to trust Him in all things. Often special holiday celebrations, like Labor Day, 5th of July (Venezuelan Independence Day), or other historic celebrations were used to protest against the institute. They even tried to use witchcraft curses against us, but to no avail.

CFM in Action

As we were in a strategic area for a Missionary Training Institute, each student was required to have a ministry in surrounding towns. Witchcraft in this country was not only prevalent amongst the indigenous population but practiced among the civilized nationals also. For example, a nearby town had the shrine of a famous doctor who supposedly performed many miracles before and after his death. People from all over the country came to this place to pray to him for their own healing or healing of someone in their family. This was a good location for the students to minister and experience the culture.

"You are of God, little children, and have overcome them, because He who is in you is greater than he who is in the world." 1 John 4:4

An extreme spiritual battle with witchcraft was a holiday that fell on October 1st called San Benito Day. San Benito is one of their saints that they claim will bring joy and happiness. They carried his statue from one catholic church to another on this day and paraded around town carrying the statue on their shoulders and beating drums. They would stop at every house which would "reimburse" them with whiskey and had San Benito bless that house, so that they would have happiness for the rest of the year. By the end of the day, they were so drunk from all the "reimbursements," that they didn't know if they were happy or not. On this day, they tried to use witchcraft to get us to leave the country. They would call on the demons to harm us or to try to kill us hoping we would have to leave, but again, it didn't work. God protected us!

Journey into the Unknown

"No weapon formed against you shall prosper, and every tongue which rises against you in judgment you shall condemn. This is the heritage of the servants of the Lord, their righteousness is from Me," says the Lord.

Isaiah 54:17

Another part of the training at CFM was that the students spent six weeks at a tribal base with the missionaries working there during the students' summer vacation. This gave them a hands-on view of what was involved in this type ministry. I wrote the following report about institute students, Marcos and Eliana, after they visited the Piaroa village.

> *We just recently received some news from the Piaroa tribe that was a real joy to hear. The work amongst the Piaroas on the Parguaza River was started in the early 70's in the village of Pendare. From 1984 until now, the people there (in Pendare) had been alone without a missionary amongst them. In January of 2002 one of our student families spent six weeks in that area. While there they visited Pendare.*
>
> *In Pendare, the student family found the Christian Piaroa leaders continued with the teaching of the Word. They found one church leader having classes with 170 unbelievers teaching them the Word from Genesis on through the death and resurrection of our Lord. The student family observed another Piaroa church leader teaching a group of 60 Piaroa believers in a more advanced Bible study. These leaders had no idea that they were going to have visitors that day and were not doing this for a show.*

CFM in Action

Our hearts were greatly blessed with the news in this letter. It confirmed once again,

"So shall my word be that goes forth from My mouth; It shall not return to Me void, but it shall accomplish what I please, and it shall prosper in the thing for which I sent it." Isaiah 55:11

We were asked to return to the States for a couple months to attend a training seminar at New Tribes Bible Institute in Jackson, Michigan. The seminar was a refresher course about animism (the belief that objects, places, and creatures all possess a distinct spiritual essence rather than a belief in God) and the world view of different cultures. This information helped us explain the Gospel to different people groups. We attended 200 hours of classes during the five-week seminar. After that, we returned to CFM with the material. After it was translated into Spanish, Fred taught it to the staff and students in the technical phase of the training. The former graduates were asked to come back for a four-week extensive course.

Class in CFM

Our remaining time at CFM, before our last furlough, Fred taught full time the third-year course. He also trained staff members to take over responsibilities. We had a Venezuelan director, Luis Jaspe, and most of the staff were Venezuelans which was another long-time goal achieved.

Journey into the Unknown

While Fred was teaching full time, he helped our field leaders and a security specialist conduct a study of the Puerto Ordaz area since we had lived there from 1985 to 1990. Based on the findings, it was apparent there was an increased threat of guerrilla activity moving into Venezuela. Puerto Ayacucho and TamaTama were more dangerous every day. Our mission needed to make some major moves. The first step was to move our main office from Puerto Ayacucho to Puerto Ordaz, ten hours away. The office had been in Puerto Ayacucho since 1946, so this was a major undertaking. Then we moved the school for missionaries' children from TamaTama to Puerto Ordaz. This was a safer location further away from the guerilla activities.

Bronco Loaded for Trip

To assist in these moves, we made several sixteen-hour trips from the Betijoque CFM school to Puerto Ordaz. The first trip was to take the mission security specialist to check out the area for an appropriate place to move and to find places to move the office and staff. The second trip was made to find homes and a storage building where the people, who would be moving there, could store their belongings until they could find a house. In Puerto Ordaz, they found a large house with five bedrooms for the first round of staff to use for temporary housing and a temporary office until they could relocate to a long-term house or office. Upon returning to Betijoque, we packed up some of the things in

CFM in Action

our house so that another family could live in it while we were on home assignment for six months.

Shortly after our return from the States, the field leadership asked if we would be willing to move back to Puerto Ordaz. They asked Fred if he would help wherever necessary in getting established there and that he be available for any government issues. Also, with the mission headquarters located there, it was more important than ever to have closer contact with the churches again.

This move involved a couple trips to Puerto Ordaz to look for a house to rent and start the government paperwork. On one of the trips, we were told about a Venezuelan family moving to Spain for three years to start a business there. They were looking for a family to rent their house while they were out of the country. That was close to the amount of time that we planned on remaining in the country. We decided to rent their house.

First CFM Graduates

It was interesting to see how the Lord led us through the years. We found ourselves moving back to Puerto Ordaz. This was the same city where we started after leaving the tribe. Promoting missions in the local churches was a burden on our hearts over the past 15 years. When we moved to the CFM Institute, the ministry in the churches practically came to a standstill. We felt our reason for being

Journey into the Unknown

at the institute was accomplished and the remaining time in the country should be dedicated to this ministry again.

It was with mixed emotions that we finally left CFM. After many years of praying, seeking, and searching, God had led us to CFM, and now He was leading us elsewhere. We reminisced about how far CFM had come from the first time we saw it and all that God had done to bring it to where it was. We remembered all the people the Lord sent to help every step of the way. The staff and students had planned a very special and emotional farewell for us. It was hard to keep the tears back as different ones expressed what we meant in their lives and how thankful they were for CFM. We went away with a song on our hearts, "To God be the Glory, great things HE hath done."

Fred Marrying Student Couple

Another special blessing to Fred and me from CFM were the marriages of three of the couples who had gone through CFM training. They wanted Fred to perform their ceremonies, and with great joy he did. All three couples are active in the ministry, and we are so thankful for this. Then, we were blessed yet again to be present for the third graduating class from CFM. Another group of Venezuelans were prepared to work in the harvest fields.

"So, Jesus said to them again, "Peace to you! As the Father has sent Me, I also send you." John 20:21

Chapter 21 – The Final Lap of this Journey

Our children were grown now. Brian was married with children in Indiana, and Melanie was working and building her life there also. Most missionaries in Venezuela our age had already gone back to the U.S. For several years, our children had asked when we would be coming back home to stay. They hinted at the inevitable; we were not getting any younger! We could also see the effect it had on our grandchildren, as they did not really know us as their grandparents. We wanted to be with our children and grandchildren and be a part of their lives and that was their desire also.

We went on a scheduled six-month home assignment in December of 2002, and we talked with our mission leadership and our children about retiring from the ministry in Venezuela. At that time, we did not know exactly what we would do when we returned to the U.S. or where we would live. We did not want to go to the "rocking chair." One thing we did know for sure was that we did not want to retire from the ministry until the Lord retired us. After much thought, discussion, and prayer, we promised our children that we would return to the States in 2005. That would give us a couple more years before making that final move.

After we returned to Puerto Ordaz from home assignment, we grew intensely aware of the guerilla activities and the worsening of the political climate. We could see the writing on the wall. Our new goal now was to ensure we left the

The Final Lap of this Journey

Venezuelans with skills to keep their ministry going without us.

We settled in our new location in Puerto Ordaz and met with our field leadership to draw up a strategy. Our ministry was to challenge the churches in the area to become self-sufficient in reaching tribal people not just in their country but in all the world (Mark 16:15). Now that we had an Institute (CFM), they could send their members to receive specialized training for this purpose. Our responsibility was to meet with groups of pastors to educate them about this training and tribal evangelism. This was basically what we were doing before we went to CFM.

As we became settled in and made contact again with the national churches, we found them more excited about sending prospective students to CFM now that it was here in the same country. During this time, as students graduated from the CFM institute and before they went to a tribe, they would stay in our home to go over the field manual. We also acquainted them with field operating policies (bookkeeping, do's and don'ts, home assignments, etc.) and many other topics that would be helpful for them to know when living in a very isolated place. One thing the men wanted to know was how to build a house in the jungles using materials found there. Fred had experience in this and was able to give them ideas on how to build a simple, economical house in the jungles. I helped the women by passing on things I had learned while living and raising children there. I also offered good tips on food preservation and tried to answer all their questions. We also tried, whenever possible, to meet the pastors and families of the future students and missionaries. This helped us get to know them better and for them to know where their young people would be going and what they would be learning.

We continued to have contact with CFM at Betijotue. As we made trips for mission conferences in nearby cities, we spent some time visiting everyone at CFM. Once, on a trip to CFM, we had what was one of the scariest incidents in all our traveling. We were making good time driving along an isolated road lined with thick trees and undergrowth. Suddenly, the car started fishtailing, and Fred worked hard to keep it on the road. He quickly realized we had a flat tire in the middle of nowhere. While Fred was preparing to change the tire, two men walked out from behind the bushes. They took us by surprise, and we were concerned about what they were up to as each one had long machetes in their hands. I was sitting in the car and immediately knew that I needed to pray for Fred and his safety. The two men came up to where Fred was unloading the car to get the spare tire out. They asked if they could help, and he felt it was best to let them help rather than to say no. I could see them clearly and could see that they were continually looking inside the car. Fred noticed this also and thought it strange. We do not know what they were looking at, but they helped change the tire. Fred gave them both a very generous tip for helping him, and they turned around and went back into the bushes. We gave a huge sigh of relief when we were safely on our way again and thanked the Lord for our protection.

Later, as we recounted this incident to some of our Venezuelan friends, they told us it was a miracle that we were not robbed and killed. It was a known fact that on that road, people hid in the bushes, and when they saw a car

The Final Lap of this Journey

coming from a distance they would throw out a strip with nails in it. They would then come out of the bushes, rob them, take their car and kill them. We think another story of an incident might explain how we were protected. A pastor told of a time his wife had dropped off several young people after church. One of the church members saw her on the road with another car suspiciously following, but her car was full of people, so they didn't stop her. When they asked her about it later, she assured him that there was no one else in the car; that she was on her way back after dropping all the young people off. The Pastor and his wife were convinced that God allowed the ones wanting to do harm to her to see a car full of people. After hearing this, we wondered...could that have been the same thing that happened to us as we both noticed how much the two men kept looking inside our car? We do not know, but it once again brought this verse to our mind.

"For He shall give His angels charge over you. To keep you in all your ways." Psalm 91:11

As mentioned earlier, the school for missionaries' children that was in TamaTama had been moved to Puerto Ordaz. The school was called Robert Shaylor Academy. They received a threatening letter from local government officials indicating they were going to close the school until they acquired the proper government permits. Fred, along with the field chairman and school director, spent some time in a lawyer's office trying to resolve the problem. After checking into it, they found that the school hadn't been registered properly after the move to Puerto Ordaz. It turned out there was a lot of work to do to allow the school to continue. This was different than living in the jungles where no government permits were needed. There were certainly a lot of adjustments to city life that we all had to make. We had learned repeatedly, many times the hard way, that God in His faithfulness had brought our mission through it all. This continued to strengthen our faith and prepared us for the hardest part which was still ahead.

Our last year in Venezuela, 2005, was full of preparing others to take over the representation work. We were thankful that two Venezuelan missionary families, the Britos and Pizzaros were added to the representation team. They traveled together with Fred as he went from one side of the country to the other. These trips were a continuation of our two-fold project to prepare the churches through conferences, seminars and special mission meetings with pastors.

One more trip was made to the grasslands, this time with the new representation team. When the people heard that this was Fred's last trip, they planned a special celebration. The ten churches in that area had gotten together and planned to give Fred a plaque of appreciation for having helped them. This was a total surprise to Fred and something that really touched him as these church leaders, having very little resources, had traveled to the nearest town to have the plaque made, paid for it themselves, and then traveled back for the presentation. We were blessed to know the impact that we had on these lives. For Fred this made all the hardships on these trips worth everything. In another town, at the end of a weekend of meetings, the church presented Fred with a Venezuelan painting by a local artist with signatures of all the church members on the

The Final Lap of this Journey

back of the painting. Their way of showing appreciation for our ministry with them was touching.

Before leaving Venezuela, our hearts were blessed and challenged afresh after attending a World Missions Congress with several of our co-workers held in the beautiful city of Merida in the Andes Mountains. It brought back many memories of the challenging messages we heard growing up that moved us to surrender our lives to the ministry. They challenged us anew over 45 years later.

The highlight of our time there was the surprise visit of eight Piaroas from the village of Punta Piaroa where we first started our ministry. They made a 3-day river trip and then a 30-hour bus ride to get there. One was the sister of Bautista, the leader of the village and the first believer in the tribe. When she heard that we were going to be there, she asked her children to take her there to see us one more time. A couple of the others had been young children in loincloths in the early 60's with no means of learning how to read and write until the missionary came to their village. One of these, was a young fellow that continued his education after moving out of the tribe and into the city where he could get advanced education. He was attending a University in Merida where he was studying to be a pharmacist. We never imagined that this little village boy would ever advance to that level. Since then, we have heard of one that is a lawyer, several became pastors in cities outside of their tribal areas. There have been several that went to CFM to prepare to go and teach in different tribes.

On our way back home, and only hours from Merida, we went by CFM to say our goodbyes to the staff and students there. Once again, our emotions were taxed to the fullest as

Journey into the Unknown

the memories came flooding back of what God had accomplished through the school. Two student families said to us, "It is your 'fault' we are here and thank you for not giving up on us." It was our "fault," because we had encouraged them to come and encouraged them to get through the tough times. That was more than thanks to us, it was part of the many rewards we received during our ministry.

Upon returning to Puerto Ordaz, we had to speed up our packing. The mission lawyer called Fred and Marcos to his office. He told them that things were looking bad for the mission and that he feared that the time for the mission there would be short. He advised Fred to consider leaving as soon as possible. We also learned that we personally had been under surveillance for the past 30 years. They had been looking for something to justify deporting us.

The Last Goodbye

As we packed and eliminated 45 years of belongings, we were honored with two surprise farewells. One was in our new mission headquarters in Puerto Ordaz. All of the mission staff that had been relocated there, and others visiting, surprised us by tricking us to go to the headquarters. When we arrived, the room was packed with co-workers who shouted "Surprise!" It truly was! They gave us a gift of an engraved pewter tray which we have to this day. The inscription on it is 'O, taste of the Lord for He is good.' What a true testimony that is of what we experienced many times.

The other surprise was at the Iglesia Evangelica Bautista "Bethel." This was one of the first churches that we had

The Final Lap of this Journey

contact with when we moved to Puerto Ordaz in the mid 80's. Fred and Marcos Brito, one of our Venezuelan representatives, were involved in the yearly mission conference. When we arrived at the church for the final service, they met us at the door and ushered us to special seats in the back of the church. Oddly, we were seated behind a pillar which blocked our view. They told us to sit in the two middle chairs with empty ones on each side. We thought this strange, as we could hardly see what was going on at the front. They went ahead with their regular service with other missionaries speaking. Then the pastor said they wanted to recognize the many years that the Findleys had served in Venezuela and then told about our leaving in May. They had a lot of chairs up on the platform, and they started calling different pastors from that area to come forward; around ten pastors. Among the chairs on the platform were two empty ones. Then they called us to come up, and as we did, the people all stood up and started clapping.

After we were seated in the two empty chairs, the pastor said they had a surprise for the Findleys. He gave a short introduction of who we were and then called his wife to come and speak. She read a brief written history of our lives and family. In it she told about the death of Dad Findley in the plane crash in 1967 and that he was buried in Puerto Ayacucho. She also told about Mother Findley staying on for many years and how she had continued the ministry they were involved in. She told about my family and about their deaths over a period of five consecutive years (1990-1994). She told about our children and how they spent all their years in the jungles until they graduated from high school, and then their separation from us when they returned to the U.S. to further their education. She also read about our grandchildren and how much we had been separated from them. Several times her voice broke as she read about our lives.

They presented us with a beautiful, gold-plated dish, which we have to this day. Then the big surprise! Three Piaroa villagers from Caño Pendare walked up front. Ramon and his wife were one of the first believers in that village. With them was a younger Piaroa that knew Spanish and did the translation for them. Ramon gave his testimony of how we went to Pendare and took God's Word to them. How he became a believer and had been faithful all these years. His wife also said a few words, with more than two-hundred people in the audience, despite her fear of speaking in public. They told of how another church leader wanted to come, but he was on a missionary trip to another village to teach. However, he wrote a letter that our co-worker, Larry Bockus, went up front and read in both Piaroa and in Spanish. He had a few words also about what we meant to them and how the Lord had used us in their lives.

Fred was asked to say a few words. Heavy with emotion, he expressed our appreciation for what they did and for the joy it had been for us to be able to spend many years there serving the Lord. He also told how hard it was for him to think of leaving, but God had given him peace about it. He expressed how we were leaving a piece of our heart

Final Goodbyes

The Final Lap of this Journey

there in Venezuela and our desire was that the evangelical church would continue to grow in their missionary vision. After all that, all the pastors circled around us and prayed for us. They all gave us hugs, and then the church choir made a half circle in front of us and sang, "God be with You till We meet again." We left the church with wet handkerchiefs, and very thankful hearts.

The last couple months in Venezuela, a country we loved, and which became a part of our lives, were very emotional for us. Just before leaving we were asked by our field chairman, if we would try and return several times a year to encourage the national and Piaroa churches. This was our plan and desire if the Lord allowed us to do so. However, this was not possible as after we left, they expelled our mission from Venezuela. Another request was made to us by the national pastors and Christian leaders. They asked if we would write a book about our many years of spreading the Gospel there and the lives it changed. This, along with many requests down through the years from different ones from both countries, was the seed planted that grew to this end. As we left, we could truly say, "Thank you, God, for giving us the privilege of serving You in Venezuela and for Your faithfulness to us."

Journey into the Unknown

Epilogue

Where do we go from here? We talked about this with our children and Fred's mother, as we faced the reality of our age and the many years of separation from our families. Our desire was to be closer to them and to spend time with our grandchildren. We both went to Venezuela at young ages, Fred as an m.k. with his parents and myself as a single lady in my early twenties. Since that time, my parents and siblings have passed away. Our children, grandchildren, and Fred's mother were the only immediate family we had when we left Venezuela.

The situation in Venezuela was declining with a resurgence of false accusations and threats of expelling the mission from the country. Fred, along with Marcos Brito, was advised by the mission lawyer that he should get out of the country as soon as possible. Due to the many years Fred had been there and being well known, the lawyer thought he would be one they would want to go after. Thus, began our unexpected exodus from the country.

As the reality of what we just heard set in, we were flooded with questions. What do we do now? Where are we going to live? We were already signed up for a place in the mission retirement homes in Florida for when we were ready, but we were not ready! Do we have to go to a "rocking chair?" We had more questions than answers. We loved the idea of the Florida weather, but we had a very strong drawing towards Indiana where our children and grandchildren lived. As we prayed about this, we witnessed another answer to prayer like many we have seen through the years. As we drove into Indianapolis to our children's

Journey into the Unknown

house, I saw some trailers and small houses for rent. The thought went through my mind, maybe we could rent something like that. Little did I know the importance of "location, location, location!" We continued to look, learn and pray for God's leading for a more permanent place while we were staying in our daughter's spare room.

The Lord provided a fine Christian realtor who worked relentlessly to find us a home. He found just the right house at just the right time. God also provided a long-time supporter of our ministry who loaned us the finances to pay for the house within our means. He supplied the willingness of our children and others to help in a needed remodeling and advising us in so many ways. God always provided much more than what we could ask or think.

Much to our joy, we were able to work as Mission Representatives for the mid-west area at the mission's request. This was mainly to the English-speaking churches and Christian colleges in Indiana, Ohio and Michigan. The desire to work with Hispanic churches was still deep in us.

In December 2011, after 52 years of full-time service, we officially retired from NTM and felt that the time was finally here to start something with the Spanish speaking churches of Indianapolis. Our desire was not to start a new church but work with, encourage, and be a help to those churches already in existence. As we began visiting churches in the area, we found a need amongst the pastors to have someone mentor them, to answer their questions and help them resolve problems. Being a pastor can be a very lonely life sometimes with no one that you can share your burdens with while many bring theirs to you. This was the opportunity that God gave us to come along side these pastors as someone they could talk with and share their burdens.

Over the following years, as we fellowshipped and encouraged the Hispanic churches and pastors, God gave us favor with them. We now have in Indianapolis, a Hispanic Pastors Fraternity of good, fundamental churches. We are working with eight groups and have been truly blessed by them. What does the future hold? Only God knows. We thank Him for the opportunity He has given us these past several years to serve Him in this ministry.

As to what has been happening in Venezuela since we left, things politically have deteriorated greatly. This has caused a real opening in the evangelical churches and they have been growing in numbers and spiritual growth. In the Piaroa church they have continued their outreach with one young family going to missionary training and now working as part of a team reaching another tribal language group. Three of Bautista's sons, Fred's translation helper, have moved to the city of Puerto Ayacucho and have started a thriving multi-language church. Several young Piaroas have graduated from the university as lawyers and are now working in that profession. Several have become teachers and education supervisors. "To God be the Glory, great thing He hath done".

We are so thankful "For the Privilege of having taken this journey" by God's Grace!

Made in the USA
Middletown, DE
05 June 2019